PRAISE FOR *WHEN*

"The biblical exposition is creative and substantive, making it an enjoyable reading experience. Dr. Grier's transparency about his own personal pilgrimage brings a rich bonus to this opportunity to grow in grace."

—Chaplain Barry Black,
United States Senate

"This is a must-read! Dr. Grier speaks about personal accounts of his life and keeping faith in God. I personally related my life's journey with God as a child being raised by a single parent and a United States Marine for thirty-six years to Dr. Grier's personal accounts. Dr. Grier's book possesses a genuine transparency that resonates through his personal walk with God."

—Carlton W. Kent, 16th Sergeant
Major of the Marine Corps

"I have known Dr. Derek Grier for more than twenty years. He lives what he preaches and preaches what he lives. He is destined to become one of the major biblical voices who speaks to the 'now generation.' More specifically, this book contains a special mixture of the Grier secret sauce—his amazing teaching gift, personal transparency, humility, and faith. Preaching from a church prophetically named Grace Church, Dr. Grier will help any Christian attract the favor of God, embrace personal transformation, develop his or her gifts, and advance the Kingdom of God. This is a must-read."

—Bishop Harry Jackson, president
of the High Impact Coalition

"It was very good. Thoroughly enjoyed it."

—Cathy Hughes, founder and
chairperson of Radio One, Inc.

"*When God Stops* falls into a category of its own. Dr. Derek Grier skillfully dissects the extraordinary God-encounters of eight ordinary men and women in the Bible. He brings the Word to life by strategically comparing their experiences to his own personal journey. The book also challenges readers to recognize God-encounters in their everyday lives and to never give up. Outstanding!"

—Pastor John K. Jenkins, First
Baptist Church of Glenarden,
Upper Marlboro, Maryland

"The ministry of Grace Church and Dr. Derek Grier has made a profound impact on the Dumfries community. I highly recommend you read *When God Stops*. Dr. Grier's story will encourage you to look over your life and recognize the many instances (good or bad) where you made God stop."

—Derrick Wood, mayor of
Dumfries, Virginia

"Dr. Derek Grier has written a powerful book focusing on people who were able to get God to stop. This book offers new perspective on familiar scriptural stories, with lessons we can use to have greater success in our daily lives. This book will inspire and empower you. I recommend you read it and then share it with your network. You will be glad you did!"

—Dr. Willie Jolley, international
motivational speaker

"Throughout history even the greatest saints have struggled with times of great difficulty and sorrow—times when despite their desperate need, God seemed to 'pass them by.' Dr. Derek Grier skillfully reminds us that our compassionate High Priest always has His gentle hand on the pulse of our lives, and in His own time will respond in glorious ways to those who refuse to give up! This is a book well worth reading and sharing with others!"

—Don Kroah, D.Min., host of *The
Don Kroah Show*, WAVA Radio

"What an incredible thought, God stopping for us! When I think of that it just blows my mind. Recently, my son, who is in Bible college, called me up spur of the moment and said, 'Dad, can you drive up to my school and watch the Dallas Cowboys game with me?' I was busy, swamped with responsibility to be honest, but I *stopped* everything, got in the car, and went to spend that day with my boy. Everything else had to wait. Why? I love my son and I would drop anything for him. In the same way, God loves us but times infinity. This book by Dr. Grier will inspire you and deepen your relationship with our heavenly Father, who loves to STOP for us."

—Frank Santora, lead pastor, Faith
Church, New Milford and Waterbury,
CT; Harlem NYC; and Duluth, GA

"Those who know Dr. Grier can give testimony to his impeccable character and how the grace of God is active in his life and his ministry. His ability to teach the Word of God in a manner that people understand, and his ability to communicate the steps about biblical living to achieve a better relationship with God is admirable. This book is a great example. This book gives the reader the opportunity to receive important keys to unlock the power to God in their life and live the life that God's grace makes available."

—Otoniel Font, senior pastor,
Iglesia Fuente de Agua Viva

"I loved it! This powerful book is as thought provoking as its unique title. Bishop Grier has managed to shift my paradigm from a person trying to get God started to a person trying to get God to stop. He teaches us that our God has the ability to work miracles, but do we have the faith to get His divine attention? Read and let your faith soar!"

—Bishop Courtney McBath, senior
founding pastor, Calvary Revival
Church, Norfolk, Virginia

"Derek Grier takes his readers on a journey to better understand themselves and their relationship with God. He adds a fresh twist by helping us see the awakening faith in those who made a request of God. As you read this work, see God at work in your life in all your critical moments."

—Bishop Walter Thomas, New Psalmist
Baptist Church, Baltimore, Maryland

"Dr. Derek Grier is a man of humble beginnings who discovered early in life the importance of putting God first. Our world is desperately in need of models worth following. Authentic heroes, people of integrity, whose lives inspire us to do better, to climb higher, to stand taller."

—Benson M. Karanja, Ed.D. H.S.C.,
president, Beulah Heights University

"It is heartwarming to meet an author who can so effectively mine the good news from Scripture. Derek Grier helps to translate the relevancy of God's power in man's every step—striking a balance of His sovereign nature with His gift of free will to humanity. *When God Stops* is certain to stir a groundswell, placing a magnifying glass on the readers' pursuit of God's purpose and destiny in their lives. I closed the book remembering that *with* God anything is possible."

—Damon Davis, president and
CEO, The Legacy Worldwide
Group of Companies

WHEN
GOD
STOPS

WHEN GOD STOPS

FAITH THAT GETS GOD'S ATTENTION

DEREK GRIER

EMANATE

BOOKS

Published in Nashville, Tennessee, by Emanate Books, an imprint of Thomas Nelson. Emanate Books and Thomas Nelson are registered trademarks of HarperCollins Christian Publishing, Inc.

Thomas Nelson titles may be purchased in bulk for educational, business, fund-raising, or sales promotional use. For information, please e-mail SpecialMarkets@ThomasNelson.com.

ISBN 978–1–4002–1289–7 (eBook)
ISBN 978–1–4002–1356–6 (TP)

Library of Congress Control Number: 2019937146

Printed in the United States of America
19 20 21 22 23 LSC 10 9 8 7 6 5 4 3 2 1

This book is dedicated to my mother, Jeanette Grier. Thank you for always caring. Only your grace exceeds your beauty. Your love always matters to me. Dad, after all these years, you are still my hero.

My heart, Yeromitou, I love you more than life itself!

DJ and David, a father could not be prouder!

Grace Church, I could not serve a finer group of people than my Grace Church family. Thank you for your constant prayers and love.

CONTENTS

FOREWORD

Derek Grier made God stop!

Rather than being an arrogant statement, it is quite the opposite. It is humbling to know that the Creator of this universe would stop for Derek and would stop for you. He did. He does. He will continue to stop. His stopping for His creation is what makes Him God.

In this book my friend Bishop Derek Grier looks at people, places, and events and unfolds how God stopped repeatedly. None of those anticipated His stopping, and yet He did.

I was intrigued by God's footprints in Bishop Grier's life. The challenges of early childhood, higher education, responding to God's call, uncertainties of leadership, fulfilled vision while lacking commensurate resources, leading while in self-doubt, trusting Him in the dark places and spaces of life, and knowing that when you can't track Him you can trust Him. God still stops.

There is no way you will read this book and not have to put it down so through teary eyes of gratefulness you can say, *"Thank you for stopping for me."* Bishop Grier's life stories and other biblical personalities highlighted in this book will serve as catalysts for pushing the Rewind button on our lives and shouting, "Hallelujah!"

Even as I write this foreword I'm reminded of a hymn of the church I grew up singing. A hymn written in 1897 by Johnson Oatman Jr. to encourage us to count our blessings because God stopped for us. Even though you might be familiar with the song, take a moment to read it out loud.

When upon life's billows you are tempest tossed,
When you are discouraged, thinking all is lost,
Count your many blessings, name them one by one,
And it will surprise you what the Lord hath done.

Count your blessings, name them one by one;
Count your blessings, see what God hath done;
Count your blessings, name them one by one;
Count your many blessings, see what God hath done.

Are you ever burdened with a load of care?
Does the cross seem heavy you are called to bear?
Count your many blessings, ev'ry doubt will fly,
And you will be singing as the days go by.

When you look at others with their lands and gold,
Think that Christ has promised you His wealth untold;
Count your many blessings, money cannot buy
Your reward in heaven, nor your home on high.

So, amid the conflict, whether great or small,
Do not be discouraged, God is over all;
Count your many blessings, angels will attend,
Help and comfort give you to your journey's end.

Bishop Grier's seminal message in this book is that if God stopped for these people in the Bible, if He stopped for the author of this book, surely He will stop for you too. He is closer than your next breath. He awaits your whisper. He wants to stop. He will stop.

Thank you, Bishop Grier, for your transparency that brings us encouragement, strength, and hope.

Sam Chand

A man for whom God stopped

INTRODUCTION

I was having lunch in Baltimore with a leading bishop. During the meal he asked me to tell my story. The question made me a little uncomfortable, but I told him about my journey. Several hours passed and by the end of the conversation, he told me to write down the things we discussed. I politely told him one day I would, but I thought to myself, *People live busy lives. Why would anyone be interested?*

Not long after that, I was at lunch with another leading religious figure, and he asked me the same question. I was a little embarrassed. I did not think this outgoing and extremely accomplished individual would be able to identify with my struggles, but I took a breath and shared my story. When our conversation ended, he told me he believed the Lord wanted me to write down what we had discussed. I explained my schedule did not allow me to do this, but maybe I would find some time in the future.

Instead of taking my friends' advice, I began writing eight practical messages that would help my congregation discover how to unlock God's power in their lives. When I completed the rough draft, I asked my wife to read it. I had not shared with her my earlier lunch conversations. She told me she enjoyed it, but she asked the same question as the others: Where was my story?

A few weeks later my wife and I were having lunch with an evangelist. Out of nowhere, she asked me to tell my story. I shared many of the points I had shared with the others. She then told both my wife and me that I needed to write these things down.

The pages ahead were written for people like myself, who at times don't feel they measure up, people who wake up and go to sleep every day dogged by the same internal conflicts, and people who feel pinned down by the weight of circumstances beyond their control. This book is about eight people in sacred history who had Jesus stop for them to address some major issues in their lives. It is also my story of how Jesus stopped for one of the least likely persons you could imagine: me.

It's my goal that you will come to know these men and women and allow them to become personal coaches and friends. We will dig into each story line by line to help you not only discover why God stopped for these eight but how God stopped for me and how to position yourself for God to stop for you today.

ONE

THE WOMAN WHO MADE GOD STOP

Now when Jesus had crossed over again by boat to the other side, a great multitude gathered to Him; and He was by the sea. And behold, one of the rulers of the synagogue came, Jairus by name. And when he saw Him, he fell at His feet and begged Him earnestly, saying, "My little daughter lies at the point of death. Come and lay Your hands on her, that she may be healed, and she will live." So Jesus went with him, and a great multitude followed Him and thronged Him.

Now a certain woman had a flow of blood for twelve years, and had suffered many things from many physicians. She had spent all that she had and was no better, but rather grew worse. When she heard about Jesus, she came behind Him in the crowd and touched His garment. For she said, "If only I may touch His clothes, I shall be made well."

Immediately the fountain of her blood was dried up, and she felt in her body that she was healed of the affliction. And Jesus, immediately knowing in Himself that power had gone out of Him, turned around in the crowd and said, "Who touched My clothes?"

But His disciples said to Him, "You see the multitude thronging You, and You say, 'Who touched Me?'"

And He looked around to see her who had done this thing. But the woman, fearing and trembling, knowing what had happened to her, came and fell down before Him and told Him the whole truth. And He said to her, "Daughter, your faith has made you well. Go in peace, and be healed of your affliction."

While He was still speaking, some came from the ruler of the synagogue's house who said, "Your daughter is dead. Why trouble the Teacher any further?"

As soon as Jesus heard the word that was spoken, He said to the ruler of the synagogue, "Do not be afraid; only believe." And He permitted no one to follow Him except Peter, James, and John the brother of James. Then He came to the house of the ruler of the synagogue, and saw a tumult and those who wept and wailed loudly. When He came in, He said to them, "Why make this commotion and weep? The child is not dead, but sleeping."

And they ridiculed Him. But when He had put them all outside, He took the father and the mother of the child, and those who were with Him, and entered where the child was lying. Then He took the child by the hand, and said to her, "Talitha, cumi," which is translated, "Little girl, I say to you, arise." Immediately the girl arose and walked, for she was twelve years of age. And they were overcome with great amazement. But He commanded them strictly that no one should know it, and said that something should be given her to eat.

(MARK 5:21–43)

S ome people may think they don't need God because of their status in society, achievements, wealth, or cultural background. Others recognize their need but feel they are not deserving enough. They ask, Why would a powerful and all-knowing God be interested in a relationship with someone as insignificant as me?

In this chapter we are going to read about two people who fit both these descriptions: a man named Jairus and a sick woman who were willing to humble themselves to receive a healing touch from Jesus. They are two unlikely characters: one from society's elite class and the other a social outcast. The man was very well-connected, respected, and influential; and the woman was disconnected, disregarded, and insignificant. They were two very different people with different problems, but they were experiencing similar levels of desperation and determination.

Jairus is a classic example of how a humble but steady hand can bring about the fulfillment of God's promise. The unnamed woman is a remarkable example of how far determination and persistence can take us. So what did a powerful synagogue leader and a shunned woman do to make God stop for them?

Now when Jesus had crossed over again by boat to the other side

Jesus crisscrossed the Sea of Galilee throughout His nearly three and a half years of ministry. What's amazing is that the man who in the pages ahead would turn water into wine, walk on water, and demonstrate

Himself to be even greater than angels, would take part in such a mundane and unspectacular mode of transportation as riding in a boat. Jesus was a man with no shortage of talents. His supernatural insights and power were off the charts. He could have done or become anything He wanted, but to truly walk among us, He had to first humble Himself to live beside us (Leviticus 26:12).

C. S. Lewis said, "Humility is not thinking less of yourself, it's thinking of yourself less."[1] Human prestige and power were not important to Jesus. His message in the Gospels is simple: God became one of us to reach us and concretely demonstrate what it truly means to live. His adaptation to human form required radical humiliation. He added humanity to deity and chose to share all our creaturely weaknesses while never for a moment giving up His unique and divine identity.

A great multitude gathered to Him; and He was by the sea.

When Jesus stepped out of the boat, a crowd swarmed around Him. He often resisted public attention by pulling aside to be alone with His Father and choosing less conspicuous settings (Luke 5:15–16; John 7:4). By this point in His ministry, however, He was an emerging religious superstar, and anonymity was difficult.

Miracles were rarely seen in Israel after the destruction of the first temple. It was impossible to work miracles of the magnitude and regularity as Christ did without drawing a considerable crowd. Yet He masterfully resisted the temptation to allow personal validation to come from the size of the crowd instead of the God within.

Jesus spoke everywhere He went, but no matter how many hours He spent enlightening the masses, they could not get enough. People were so hungry for His message that they would often follow Him for days without eating or resting. Though His pace was grinding, He never grew irritated or scolded anyone for their hunger. He only scolded those who lacked it. Mother Teresa observed, "A hunger for love is a thousand times harder to remove than a hunger for bread."[2] Jesus understood this, and this was the very reason He came (John 6:35).

And behold, one of the rulers of the synagogue came, Jairus by name.

Out of the crowd came an improbable man, a synagogue leader. Such men were extremely powerful and an important part of the ruling class. They tended to be some of the most intelligent, educated, and influential people in their communities.

This synagogue ruler, Jairus, wielded tremendous respect and fear. His authority could be compared to that of a big city mayor today but with the extraordinary power of excommunication. Exercising this power could mean ostracism and poverty. The mild form banned the excommunicated from coming within six feet of another Jew, including his or her own family, and lasted a minimum of thirty days.[3] In more severe cases, excommunication could mean the permanent loss of all family contact. The excommunicated person could no longer conduct business with observant Jews, which often meant he had no means by which to make a living. This type of excommunication was a fate common Jews feared worse than death.

Jairus was what some today would call a shot-caller. Those who witnessed the meeting of the carpenter from Galilee and this synagogue ruler no doubt thought Jesus had more to fear from Jairus than Jairus could ever gain from Jesus. As was so often the case with Jesus, all conventional wisdom was about to get turned upside down.

And when he saw Him

It's likely Jairus was a Pharisee, as were most synagogue leaders of that time. Jesus was crossing lines, making statements, and taking actions unlike anyone who preceded Him. Jesus had quickly become the center of heated religious debate. No doubt, Jairus was familiar with the controversies surrounding Him. Jairus probably disagreed with Him on many critical points, as did most of his party. When he saw Jesus, however, he was willing to look beyond their differences to discover what lay behind those piercing eyes.

Jairus had lived as a student of Scripture. The fulfillment of more than fifteen hundred years of Jewish prophecy had just stepped out of a boat and into his view. The Word of God had become flesh. As the young carpenter stood there, everything else that had seemed important began to shrink, including Jairus's culturally ingrained sense of superiority and importance. The enormity of all that was packed into a man who many anthropologists believe was only a little over five feet tall was the ultimate reality check.[4]

He fell at His feet

Ignoring the recriminations and fully understanding his actions could cost him his position and standing in his religious party, Jairus publicly fell to his knees in front of Jesus. This was a sweeping acknowledgment before everyone watching that Jesus possessed greater power and authority than even this powerful synagogue ruler.

Life had hit Jairus hard. His need was shouting a thousand times louder than his pride, which has a way of humbling us. He realized he did not have all the answers and was ready to stop pretending otherwise and begin to seek the One who did.

Jairus not only came to Jesus but knelt before Him at the expense of his reputation and everything he had worked for his whole life. Worship is more than singing a favorite gospel song, though that is a great place to start. It is our hearts' and bodies' honest response to a glimpse of the greatness of God and is usually most authentic when it costs us something (2 Samuel 24:24).

The most revealing moments are when we have to make a choice between the right thing and the easy thing. At this point in the gospel narrative, all eyes were on Jairus. The crowd was shocked. His peers were possibly disgusted. Yet Jairus was willing to surrender his ego to the awesomeness of the man who stood before him.

And [Jairus] begged Him earnestly, saying, "My little daughter lies at the point of death."

When personal tragedy strikes, petty jealousies, trivial differences, race, gender, and political affiliations lose their importance. Our priorities become clear, and the only thing that matters is resolving the crisis at hand.

It tears at our instincts about the natural order for a child to die before a parent. Nothing in life can prepare a mother or father for the agony of a moment like this. This powerful synagogue ruler was helpless. Like any loving parent, he was desperate to bring back his little girl.

"Come and lay Your hands on her, that she may be healed, and she will live."

A lifetime of reading Genesis through Malachi taught Jairus that one touch from God could change anything. Jesus appeared as a bridge between heaven and earth, life and death, and Jairus was ready to take that chance. I can't say it was specifically something he had heard Jesus say, felt in Jesus' presence, or saw in Jesus' eyes, but Jairus obviously believed that the man some were calling the Messiah would be willing to heal his daughter. Jairus was not going to let anything get in the way of that healing. Especially not his pride. If Jesus were going to help anyone, He was going to help him and his little girl on that day.

So Jesus went with him

This is important. Jesus always goes with people who are willing to trust Him. Faith can be risky, but unbelief in the face of Jesus' track record is even more dangerous. Notice that despite the antagonism of other Pharisees, Jesus did not discriminate against this Pharisee. God did not turn Jairus away because of his party affiliation, religious denomination, or past criticisms. And He won't turn you away because of yours. Jesus will walk with anyone who will humble himself and make the choice to believe.

And a great multitude followed Him and thronged Him.

The crowd was literally pushing, pulling, and tugging at Jesus from every side. It took a great deal of effort for Jesus and His disciples to walk through this crowd. Despite tremendous pressure, Jesus never allowed the crowd to dictate His teaching, agenda, or purpose.

A sea of human need pressed against Him on every side. Yet Jesus maintained His commitment to walk with Jairus. God will never leave those who don't leave Him (Hebrews 13:5).

Now a certain woman had a flow of blood for twelve years

Life seldom happens in neat compartments. While dealing with one crisis, another crisis arose. We all have had moments when life demands more from us than we think we can supply. In such times our heads can start spinning, and we are tempted to buckle under the weight of it all. We would do well, however, to learn from Jesus' example in this story.

Jesus was clear about His goal of walking with Jairus to his house, but He was flexible with the schedule. He was firm in His decision to help Jairus but open to whatever opportunities God might present along the way and was willing to adjust accordingly. The trust both this man and this woman put in Jesus was precious, sacred, and inviolable to Him. He would not disappoint either.

And had suffered many things from many physicians.

Think about the lengths we go to ensure our physical well-being. Chemotherapy and radiation treatment are just two of the extreme possibilities we may face concerning our health. The ancient medical world had equally draconian procedures designed to heal illness. Below are just a few treatments that might have been prescribed to the woman described in this passage.

Take of the gum of Alexandria, the weight of a zuzee (a fractional silver coin); of alum the same; of crocus the same. Let them be bruised together, and given in wine to the woman that has an issue of blood.

If this does not benefit, take of Persian onions three logs (pints); boil them in wine, and give her to drink, and say, "Arise from thy flux."

If this does not cure her, set her in a place where two ways meet, and let her hold a cup of wine in her right hand, and let someone come behind and frighten her, and say, "Arise from thy flux."

Let them dig seven ditches, in which let them burn some cuttings of vines, not yet four years old. Let her take in her hand a cup of wine, and let them lead her away from this ditch, and make her sit down over that. And let them remove her from that, and make her sit down over another, saying to her at each remove, "Arise from thy flux!"[5]

She had spent all that she had and was no better, but rather grew worse.

This woman had followed all the conventional wisdom of the day. She did everything the doctors told her. After years of humiliation, her situation only worsened. The treatments were expensive, which only compounded her problem with every new "miracle cure" attempt. This heartbreaking pursuit of healing from human hands ultimately left her penniless.

After twelve years of failed treatments and suffering, she finally hit bottom. The advantage of hitting rock bottom is that our only hope is to look up. The next verse was the game changer.

When she heard about Jesus

The woman had grown weaker and weaker with every attempt at a cure. Then she ran out of money. On top of this, she was ceremonially unclean (Leviticus 15:25–27). According to the Mosaic law, which governed the culture at the time, she lived in isolation because of her uncleanness. Her condition was viewed as transmittable perhaps due to the flowing nature of her monthly cycle. The result was that she made unclean anyone she touched.

The woman was isolated, hopeless, and vulnerable, but somebody had told her about Jesus! This was her last chance. When this woman heard about Jesus, she decided she would try something new and hoped that her lonely days would finally come to an end.

She hoped to not only stop her endless monthly cycle, but she hoped she would finally break the cycle of isolation that had dominated her life for so many years. But none of this could happen, unless someone cared enough to take the time and energy to tell her about Jesus (Romans 10:14).

She came behind Him in the crowd and touched His garment.

Notice that this woman came up behind Jesus, as if to sneak up on Him. It's possible she came through the area of the crowd that was the thinnest. But it is also likely that, due to her uncleanness, she came to Him from that direction because she was too ashamed to meet the young rabbi face-to-face. What is amazing about God is that no matter how bloody our unending cycles have been, His grace effortlessly swallows up the worst of our uncleanliness and never vice versa.

Considering the many years she had suffered this ongoing blood loss and the cramps that often accompany prolonged menstruation, the woman probably spent many days bent over and barely able to walk. How was she able to get through the huge crowd to touch Jesus?

Likely she covered her face and got down on her hands and knees and crawled toward him. She weaved in and out and between the legs of the crowd to get to Jesus.

As difficult as getting to Jesus was, she would not be denied. It's likely this horde stepped on her hands, kneed her in her ribs, and hit her in the head. Others may have tripped over her, some would have reprimanded her with a whack or a shove, but she was determined to get her miracle or die trying.

The woman did not have the luxury of knowing someone who could have given her a special opportunity to meet Jesus privately. So she made her own opportunity. She refused to let anything, or anyone, block her from what God had in store.

Best practices today are to wait on God to open some doors for us. But sometimes God is waiting on us to get so "sick and tired of being sick and tired" that we reach the point our cycles become so unacceptable to us that we are willing to rise up and do whatever it takes to get past the obstacles holding us back.[6] When to wait and when to push is an ever-present question, but true wisdom is knowing the difference!

For she said, "If only I may touch His clothes, I shall be made well."

It doesn't matter what people say or think about you. What matters is what God says about you and what you say or think about yourself!

This woman thought she would be healed if she could just touch Jesus' clothes. After believing it in her heart, it was only natural to do whatever it took to receive what she so deeply desired. Our problem is not that we do not believe God *can* help us but that we are not convinced, like this woman, that He *will* help us!

Obviously, it was more than her hand that touched Jesus' garments. It was her heart. It was not faith alone that caused her breakthrough; it was her faith and her actions that caused her hopes to be fulfilled.

Solomon said, "For as he thinks in his heart, so is he" (Proverbs 23:7). Because this woman stood up on the inside, she would soon be standing on the outside!

> Immediately the fountain of her blood was
> dried up, and she felt in her body that
> she was healed of the affliction.

We have talked about this woman pressing through the crowd, but first she had to press through her own crowded mind and heart. She had to get beyond all her past failures, every doubt, excuse, and imagination that told her touching Jesus would not work.

The pressure of twelve years of disappointment and discouragement weighed on her. But the seed of divine hope had been placed in her heart, and she would feed it until it leaped. After enduring the pressure, obstacles, and the long crawl, she finally made it to Jesus. She touched what most people in her circumstances would have never even dreamed about touching, but when she did, she was immediately made well. A famous industrialist once said, "Problems are only opportunities in work clothes."[7]

And Jesus, immediately knowing in Himself that power had gone out of Him, turned around in the crowd and said, "Who touched My clothes?"

The healing of the woman stopped Jesus in His tracks. Pay special attention to *who* Jesus stopped for. Remember, the Mosaic law declared the woman to be unclean. She was not to have any physical contact with anyone, which she obviously had as she pushed herself through the pressing crowd.

We are left with a startling conclusion. Jesus stopped for a person who *sinned all the way to her miracle.* Here is the lesson: Never let your sinful condition stop you from pursuing God. Your cycles and sins are no match for God's grace!

But His disciples said to Him, "You see the multitude thronging You, and You say, 'Who touched Me?'"

The disciples were clueless. They did not grasp that Jesus was not talking about just the touch of a hand but about the touch of a persevering heart. Nothing releases the power of God like persevering faith. Watch how events compound in the next few verses. Jesus not only stopped; He looked.

And He looked around to see her who had done this thing.

Just as Jesus looked for the woman who touched Him, He is still looking today for people who will let their abandon come alive in their actions. Unlike thousands of other sick women in her part of the world, the woman in this story did not just think or pray about her problem. She did something about her problem! She understood that thunder may be impressive, but lightning does all the work.[8]

But the woman, fearing and trembling, knowing what had happened to her

The woman knew her actions would be regarded as irresponsible and selfish by those she had touched on her way to Jesus. In fact, she could have been excommunicated or stoned to death for what she had done, considering the ruler of the synagogue had seen the whole thing. She was understandably afraid of what might happen next.

Had she angered Jairus by not only touching Jesus but for interrupting His critical trip to the synagogue ruler's home? Would she be punished for defying the ceremonial law of Moses? She was torn between rejoicing and running. But what happened next revealed that Jesus was not only interested in what happened in her body, He was deeply concerned about what was going on in her heart.

Came and fell down before Him and told Him the whole truth.

The secrets the woman tried to hide as she passed through the crowd, she no longer tried to hide from Jesus. Confession of our wrongs to the God who loves us is the first step in making things right (1 John 1:9). I don't advocate lying to anyone, but if I had to lie, the last person I would want to lie to is God. If anyone can handle the truth, it's the One who already knows it.

When this woman bared her soul before the entire throng, her actions became an illustration of how the law of faith trumps the laws of sin and death. As an instructor can wipe clean whatever she wants off a whiteboard, there is no stain God's hand cannot far more easily erase from our lives.

And He said to her, "Daughter"

Don't miss this! This woman could not attend the synagogue or be in physical contact with those she loved because of her uncleanness. But despite her condition and despite what others might have thought, Jesus embraced her at the highest possible level. He called her His very own daughter.

She did not become a daughter because she was perfect but because she was unrelenting. Her willingness to make a God-inspired decision and see it through, no matter the ceremonial prohibitions or cost, made her a kindred spirit with the Lord.

Your faith

Jesus certainly wasn't referring to her faith in her own goodness. Her willingness to put others in ceremonial jeopardy to get to Jesus lets us know she was not the most conscientious person who ever followed Him. Her faith, instead, had to trust entirely in the mercy and power of Jesus, not in herself.

Her example reveals that faith that releases God's power is not dependent on how good we are but exclusively on how good God is. Like this woman, we are all bleeding, crawling, and failing in some way. No human being can ever approach God based on her or his own merits or abilities.

The prophet Isaiah clearly described our condition. He said all human righteousness is but "filthy rags." The delicate reader may blush at this description, but most Bible footnotes will tell you Isaiah was referring to the type of rag used by women to dress their monthly flow, a menstruation rag. The prophet pointed out that apart from God's power we are all a bloody mess.

Like city kids leaping from one high-rise rooftop to another, if they miss the opposite rooftop by an inch or by several feet, the ensuing fall is always the same, certain death. You may be able to jump farther than I can, but what does it matter because we both fall short and are plunging toward a certain death. Unlike city buildings, the distance between our righteousness and God's is so enormous it cannot be measured by inches or feet, and for this reason God Himself came to provide us with an adequate bridge so no one ever has to plunge.

Your faith has made you well.

Here is the whole point of the narrative. This woman stopped trying to fix herself. She came to Jesus exactly as she was, endless cycle and all. Likewise, God wants us to come to Him exactly as we are, right now! Even if it means getting on our knees, we must find the courage to press through all our past failures and doubts and come to Him. It will be worth it!

Go in peace, and be healed of your affliction.

I do not believe God loved this woman any more than everyone else in the crowd. I believe Jesus did for this woman what He would do for anyone and everyone. It's not a matter of whether God wants to do great things for us but how much we are willing to trust, persevere, and risk to receive it.

While He was still speaking, some came from the ruler of the synagogue's house who said, "Your daughter is dead."

When Jairus received the news his daughter was dead, I am sure his heart leaped into his throat. Time stood still as he tried to grasp the reality of what he'd just heard. He would never see his daughter at the dinner table again. He would never give her hand in marriage, never have grandchildren who looked like her. She would never again put her hand in his. He would never feel his heart skip a beat whenever she looked into his face with her twelve-year-old trusting eyes.

Jesus had begun the journey to Jairus's home to minister to his critically ill daughter. But while they were on the way, He paused to stop and talk to an unclean woman, during which time Jairus's daughter died. We see a demonstration of the fact God loves the worst of us as much as the best of us. He loves the in-crowd as much as the out-crowd.

If Jairus were anything like me, I imagine him thinking that if Jesus had not stopped for this woman, who should never have been out of her house in the first place, his daughter might still be alive. I can imagine Jairus, folding his arms, tapping his foot, and glaring at this woman as she "told Him the whole truth," which meant she probably went on and on about her medical history and her healing.

We have, on the one hand, the unnamed woman who had bled for twelve years. On the other, we have a twelve-year-old girl near death. Some say the only thing more painful than wanting a child and not being able to have one is watching helplessly while your child suffers, withers away, and dies. God cared for both but handled their crises in His own way.

"Why trouble the Teacher any further?"

The word translated as "trouble" in Greek here denotes an intense or violent exchange. Jairus was not only grieving the loss of his daughter, he was also becoming upset with Jesus. We all have moments of frustration with God. This man would not be the first person to get angry at God's purposes—and he would not be the last.

The measure of a relationship is not so much the absence of anger between the two parties but how anger is handled when it occurs. We must learn from Jairus.

As soon as Jesus heard the word that was spoken, He said to the ruler of the synagogue, "Do not be afraid; only believe."

Jesus heard the stinging news given to Jairus. But as bad as the situation was, He asked Jairus to control his emotions. As the icy fingers of panic tried to grip him, Jairus resisted and listened to God. Jairus had to focus on the goal over the pain.

Notice that Jesus told him what not to do ("be afraid") and what to do ("only believe"). Neither directive entailed figuring everything out. Delays come not because God has rejected our faith but usually to deepen and expand it.

In situations such as this, most of us get angry and walk away from Jesus. But not Jairus. When we look back over our lives, we might notice those moments when we felt most like walking away from God were the very moments we were closest to victory. We just needed to hang on to God's promise a little longer.

And He permitted no one to follow Him except Peter, James, and John the brother of James.

Interrupted by the difficult news of the death of Jairus's daughter, Jesus encouraged the mourning father to continue the journey home. Jairus walked quietly with Jesus, following His instructions. There were no rambling words or questioning. Just a growing, quiet confidence that only those who have successfully walked with Jesus through trouble can understand.

When they arrived at the home, Jesus knew how vulnerable Jairus was. So He protected him by limiting those who had access to him. There are few things as devilishly infectious as doubt and fear. The last thing Jairus needed was the wrong group of people whispering in his ear at this crucial moment. Jesus only allowed His three most seasoned and senior disciples to accompany Him into the home.

Then He came to the house of the ruler of the synagogue, and saw a tumult and those who wept and wailed loudly.

As they approached the house, they could hear wailing from within. When Jairus entered the home, the wailing intensified, as was the custom. The scene was heartbreaking, and Jesus studied and addressed each face in the house.

When He came in, He said to them, "Why make this commotion and weep? The child is not dead, but sleeping."

It seemed this young rabbi had the worst bedside manner this family had ever seen. He dared ask why the relatives were so upset that the little girl had died. If looks could kill, Jesus wouldn't have had to wait for His crucifixion.

If this were not enough, Jesus took the added step into the absurd and told them what they were crying about was not really the case. The little girl was not dead, just sleeping. If people knew one thing for sure in this time period before hospitals and funeral parlors, it was the difference between a dead person and a sleeping person.

If this family was anything like my family, the three disciples and Jairus would have had to pull them off Jesus. The good teachers, however, are not afraid of their students. Jesus was trying to teach them something. Death may have spoken to this family, but it was only Jesus who would have the last word!

And they ridiculed Him.

After Jesus spoke, the room erupted in disrespect, laughter, and scorn. They thought the young preacher from Nazareth was out of His mind. But we are about to discover when we give even the worst situations to Jesus, some people may think it is laughable at first, but if you hang in there, you will have the last laugh in the end.

But when He had put them all outside

I need you to imagine how difficult this was. In a culture where the aged were revered, Jesus made all the grandparents leave. He also removed Uncle Sugar Ray, nephew Gunner, and Aunt She Crazy among all the other family members. Jesus evidently wasn't scared of anyone and was nobody to mess with!

He took the father and the mother of the child, and those who were with Him, and entered where the child was lying.

Jesus got rid of everyone who had laughed. Only five other individuals were in the room with Him and the little girl: the parents and the three disciples. He was not rude for the sake of being rude. It's just that you can't have positive results when constantly surrounded by negative people.

The time it would have taken Jesus to teach everyone and get that entire household on the same page would have left the girl dead for days. So it was a better use of time to make some of the people leave. Our spiritual journeys are sometimes like elevators; we must let people off before we can get to the highest floors.

No matter how hard we try, we will never make everybody happy and certainly never make everyone believe. Perhaps this is the point. Sometimes we don't need as many people as we think we need to get a job done. It's not the size of the group but the size of our faith that will make the difference.

Then He took the child by the hand, and said to her, "Talitha, cumi," which is translated, "Little girl, I say to you, arise."

Jesus had already said the little girl was not dead but sleeping. He then backed up His words with action. He grabbed her by the hand and spoke to her as if to wake her up.

Notice, in this bedroom He did not speak to God, He spoke to the young girl. Many of us are quick to speak to God about our problems, but Jesus spoke to His problems: "Little girl, I say to you." Many of us are too timid to act like Jesus in our crises and for this reason we never see Christlike results (Mark 11:23).

You may be looking at an unresponsive relationship, a lifeless dream, or a dead opportunity. Just remember you started on this journey with a Jesus who specializes in making dead things breathe again.

Immediately the girl arose and walked, for she was twelve years of age.

Right after Jesus instructed the girl to get up, she obeyed. Even the dead will do whatever the Word of God says. She not only sat up in the very place she had lain, she left her bed and walked. Jesus not only revived her but also cured her of whatever killed her in the first place.

And they were overcome with great amazement.

When those in the room saw the little girl get up and walk, they were astonished at the power of Jesus. Everyone wants an ending like this, but it came only after Jairus hung on in the middle of it. If this type of faith were easy, everyone would walk in it. As Jimmy Dugan (Tom Hanks) in *A League of Their Own* (1992) said, "The hard is what makes it great."[9]

But He commanded them strictly that no one should know it, and said that something should be given her to eat.

Jesus' relationship with the girl didn't end with the miracle. He cared enough to notice that she had not eaten for days. Jesus not only cares about the big challenges in our lives. He also cares about the small ones. He performed a miracle to raise the girl from the dead but asked people to use basic things in their power to support her and allow her to fully recover.

It would be difficult to find two more dissimilar people than the synagogue ruler and the woman with the bleeding problem. The powerful Jairus trusted Jesus during the greatest crisis of his life. The bleeding woman illegally pressed her way through an unrelenting mob to receive healing despite her own frailties and pain. These two people were from different worlds and opposite circumstances, but their lives converged due to this amazing man.

God did not choose one above the other. He stopped to meet both of their needs right where they were, and their lives were never the same again. Though there are a lot of things I will never understand about being a woman, I do understand what it is like to struggle for years with internal issues that limit a person's ability to connect socially with others. I understand what it is like to be shunned and feel locked out but still continue my painful press to get through a crowded mind to experience Him.

On the other hand, I was never as powerful as the ruler of the synagogue, nor did I have a significant religious background. But like Jairus, I have had to face my deeply entrenched hostility toward Christianity. I have had to learn to block out what others were saying and find a way to keep walking with this most unusual man, in the worst crises of my life.

My Story

As a young man I did not have much of a frame of reference for the church world except for the little I saw on television and a few church-going neighbors on my block. I attended mass with my cousins a few times and went to Sunday school with neighbors on a few occasions but was unaffected by it all. One summer, however, my mother had the wisdom to send me to a two-week Christian camp in South Jersey.

I don't remember if I was in second or third grade; I just remember it was before I moved back to New York, which happened right before fourth grade. Apart from being away from home on my own, the worst thing about the camp was the corny rhythms of church songs they constantly asked us to sing. At first I refused to join with the group in singing the camp songs. I folded my arms and watched, but after days of resisting, at the end of one particular activity-filled day, they had what they called a jamboree.

Perhaps it was the sugar high from the Fun Dip and Lik-m-Aid candy, but this evening I finally joined in. They sang several hymns, and I mouthed the words until they came to one song about the name of Jesus. The chorus went something like "Jesus, Jesus, Jesus; there's just something about that name." Then they got to the line "Kings and kingdoms will all pass away, but there's something about that name." I was no longer just going through the motions; I sang those words, and I felt a presence I could not explain.

It's hard to describe, but I felt fully known with a sense of acceptance and belonging I had never felt before. I did not become a Christian, but the moment created a sort of North Star in me that subconsciously compelled me from that day forward.

Shortly after this experience my family moved back to Long Island. My parents both grew up in the Bronx. After my father served in the air force during the Korean War, he met my mother, and they were soon married and rented an apartment in Queens. My mother worked as a receptionist at a medical center, and my father was an engineer in the Polaris missile program. Eventually they bought a house in North Babylon on Long Island, where I entered the world as their third child.

My father is a tough and outgoing man. He has one of the sharpest minds I know and is a great conversationalist. He can talk about almost any sport, politics, cars, and current events given a moment's notice. I am certain if it were willing to talk, he could start a conversation with a doorknob. My mother, on the other hand, is equally tough but sensitive and quiet. She is independent and strong willed, but she has battled severe shyness all her life. I am a combination of both my parents, but when it comes to natural shyness I am very much like my mother.

On weekends my parents almost always had friends, relatives, and neighbors over to visit. If we did not have company, we were company at someone else's house. While the adults talked, laughed, and drank, the kids were playing tag and doing the things kids do.

Some of my fondest childhood memories include the smell of cigarette smoke, the sounds of adults laughing, and R&B music. When the parties really got started, especially the ones at my grandmother's house in New York City, they would call the kids in and ask us to dance. Though I loved music, whenever they called us in, I had weird, conflicting emotions. I enjoyed being around people, but being in front of a crowd, even a small crowd of people who loved me, was excruciating.

As I child I was a chronic daydreamer and extremely introverted. Though I enjoyed people, connecting with others socially did not come easily. I was extremely uncomfortable in groups. I often had what I later discovered were panic attacks around others. I desperately tried to hide by walking off alone whenever we were someplace new. My parents encouraged me, and at other times patiently scolded me, but it didn't change my naturally withdrawn disposition.

I enjoyed athletics, but being part of a team was difficult. I learned to play basketball by playing one on one with whoever would play with me in my backyard, but I hated going out to the public courts. After a stomachache caused by anxiety, I forced myself to try out for the high school basketball team. I made the team, but playing in front of people and interacting with the other players was so uncomfortable I found a reason to quit.

I could spend time with guys on an individual basis if we had some common interest, but I was an early bloomer when it came to my interest in girls. I was a little fast for my age and tended to like older girls. The older girls, however, always had a set of older friends that ultimately led to my hanging out with people a lot older than I was. The only thing that was worth tolerating a group was a pretty girl.

Being a light-eyed kid in my neighborhood (my mother's genes), I had to quickly learn how to throw a punch as well as take one. By high school I had a reputation for having a temper and being a little crazy. I liked it, because it kept most people away from me. As I got older, I began to find myself on the wrong side of the law, in places a kid my age should not be and running with a crowd that was sometimes dangerous. It was only a matter of time before it all caught up with me.

Almost every weekend was a narrow escape—fist fights, handling weapons, driving drunk or high—and could have been life altering. The end of my sophomore year in high school, my father received a job transfer that changed my life. We moved from Central Islip to Willingboro, New Jersey. In New York I was relatively quiet. I minded my business as long as others minded theirs. No one in the neighborhood had seemed bothered by that, because they had known me to be that way since elementary school.

But starting over in high school was very difficult for me. New people sometimes misread my silence as arrogance. And I became even more withdrawn. I became darker, angrier, and lonelier.

In the evenings I walked to a park just around the corner from our house. It had a ridge at its center, and I would climb it with a pack of cigarettes in hand, as if to get within better earshot of God. I had become deeply cynical despite the many times I hummed that song I had sung in camp as a child. But I was frustrated by the fact that I never experienced that sense of belonging again. I guess in my mind, I thought that if I could not get God's positive attention, I would settle for some negative attention.

I would sit on that hill in the dark and taunt God, asking, If He were good, why is there racism, evil, and suffering? I called Him all types of names and used the foulest language, insulting God for not taking more control of this world. After I poured out my strongest arguments in the most poisonous terms, I often challenged Him, saying, "If You are really out there, show Yourself!" One night, as I poured out my disrespect, I experienced a moment that is hard to explain. For an instant, it felt as if someone was listening.

For just a moment, it felt like time had ears and heard my

every word. Considering my cocky irreverence, I knew I was writing a check I could not cash. I felt real fear, as real as if I were on a dark and dangerous street. After that, I only climbed the ridge during the day.

I am sure God and any angels paying attention that night roared with laughter as they heard this pimple-faced, self-consumed sixteen-year-old shake his fist at heaven, knowing the shaking God would give me just a few years later.

Summary

- When a crisis is severe enough, petty differences melt away and all that matters is finding help.
- Faith can be risky, but unbelief is a million times more dangerous.
- Your hunger, not your goodness, will determine your results with God.
- Even if you have to crawl, get to Jesus!
- Your sin is never a match for God's grace!

Self-Analysis

1. When have you tried to get help from the wrong source? What was the result? Was it worth it in the end? Why or why not?
2. What happened the last time you bared all before God and patiently waited on Him?
3. Have you ever had to crawl to Jesus? What happened?

4. How have you learned to put your faith in Christ and not in your own understanding?

5. What do you sense God is calling you to do today as a result of your reading? What has the approach of Jairus and the woman taught you about how to approach God?

TWO

THE MAN WHO MADE GOD LOOK UP

Then Jesus entered and passed through Jericho. Now behold, there was a man named Zacchaeus who was a chief tax collector, and he was rich. And he sought to see who Jesus was, but could not because of the crowd, for he was of short stature. So he ran ahead and climbed up into a sycamore tree to see Him, for He was going to pass that way. And when Jesus came to the place, He looked up and saw him, and said to him, "Zacchaeus, make haste and come down, for today I must stay at your house." So he made haste and came down, and received Him joyfully. But when they saw it, they all complained, saying, "He has gone to be a guest with a man who is a sinner."

Then Zacchaeus stood and said to the Lord, "Look, Lord, I give half of my goods to the poor; and if I have taken anything from anyone by false accusation, I restore fourfold."

And Jesus said to him, "Today salvation has come to this house, because he also is a son of Abraham; for the Son of Man has come to seek and to save that which was lost."

(LUKE 19:1–10)

When driving from New Jersey to lower or midtown Manhattan, most people take the tunnels. No matter how bright the day happened to be, in the 1980s, as soon as you enter the tunnel, the lighting became yellowish gray, accented by the hue of taillights. The air was thick with the smell of exhaust, burning rubber, and a dozen other hard-to-classify odors.

I would take the Lincoln or Holland Tunnels, depending on where I was trying to go. Both are only a couple of miles long. The lowest part of their walls was thick, exposed concrete that acted as embankments. The rest of the walls and ceilings were covered in what looked like bathroom tile. No matter how often I drove these tunnels, the thought always crossed my mind, *What if something happens and I get stuck down here?* But every time I entered one side of the tunnel, I made it to the other side of the Hudson. Natural light would fill my car again. The air would smell fresher, and I was ready to make my next turn.

One of these tunnels opened in the 1920s and the other in the 1930s. Both tunnels were built for utility not for comfort, to get the driver from one side of the Hudson to the other and not for warm fuzzies in the middle. In this chapter I want to talk about a man who was willing to face some personal discomfort, navigate through some dense traffic, and in the end position himself not in a high-rise but in a sycamore tree to see Jesus.

I want to show you from this narrative that passage from one side of life to the other requires some level of discomfort. But there is light at the end of your tunnel if you persevere, and there are things even the most ordinary people can do to stand out in a crowd. Zacchaeus began his search for Jesus at the bottom of the pile, but he kept his focus and transitioned to the top.

Then Jesus entered and passed through Jericho.

Archaeologists regard Jericho as one of the oldest cities in the world. The Old Testament gives us some details about its landscape: "the South, and the plain of the Valley of Jericho, the city of palm trees" (Deuteronomy 34:3). The city was known for its lush palm trees, and by the time of Christ, it was also one of the wealthiest cities in the region.

Jericho would be equivalent to Beverly Hills or Greenwich, Connecticut, or one of the other high-end zip codes in the United States. It was a magnet for the rich and famous and dotted with luxurious villas. It boasted all the luxuries and comforts the world offered at that time in history.

It was also a major border city, the home of an important Roman customs station, and a hub of the latest news and gossip. Due to its southern location and the dense traffic through the area, its residents had the first choice of the newest fashions, spices, and delicacies from Northern Africa and other parts of the Mediterranean world.

One thing often overlooked about this passage, considering the affluence of the area, is that Luke does not say Jesus came to stay in Jericho but that He "passed through" the city. This speaks volumes about Jesus. A person with the talent, personality, charisma, and power of Jesus could have easily felt entitled to stay. After all, He was human, and it would be understandable that He might pause to get some much-needed rest. But the greatest moral challenges we face are not choices between right and wrong; they are choices between God's best and what is convenient.

Jesus was less than twenty miles from the cruelest and most barbaric beatings in human history. He was facing protracted torture, public mockery, deep personal humiliation, spiritual abandonment, and death (Matthew 27:46). Nonetheless, Jesus understood there is a time for everything, including enjoying certain pleasures (1 Timothy 6:17).

What was next for Jesus required incredible toughness, and He needed to continue conditioning Himself for the assignment ahead. Progress usually begins at the end of our comfort zones. Sometimes the places where we feel most drawn to stop and rest are really traps designed to stop us. Soft people seldom have the temperaments to offer hard solutions.

Now behold, there was a man named Zacchaeus who was a chief tax collector, and he was rich.

Tax collecting for the Roman government was highly organized and extremely profitable. The senior administrator of a region was called the chief tax collector. The Romans incentivized tax collection by giving each tax collector a commission on what they collected. Above this, the chief tax collector received a percentage of all the money obtained by the tax collectors under him. Considering the volume of traffic on the trade route through Jericho, Zacchaeus had the power and wealth most people today only dream of. His lucrative profession, however, had a tragic downside: his life was an enigma.

His name means "pure," but Zacchaeus was anything but pure. He was a Jew who worked for the repressive, often brutal Roman Empire. The Jews considered him a traitor, and the Romans only used him for their own purposes. Every day he sank deeper into the cutthroat world of survival and intrigue.

Hatred of tax collectors was not without cause, because more often than not they functioned as a government-sanctioned crime syndicate. Not only did the tax collectors often appropriate part of the taxes for themselves, but they also often inflated the taxpayers' bills. As far as the average taxpayer was concerned, there was no recourse for a non-Roman against a rogue tax collector. It was commonplace for tax collectors to threaten, beat, and even imprison the weakest and most vulnerable in society to get paid.

An unpaid tax bill could easily mean incarceration and in some cases result in children being sold into slavery to satisfy the debt. This tax system was brutal but protected because it was the primary source of revenue for Rome, which needed to fund its expansive army and maintain military control over its vast territories. Zacchaeus was a willing and handsomely compensated accessory to this tyranny, and his countrymen hated him for it.

And he sought to see who Jesus was

Despite his wealth, power, and property, this hardened man had an inner hunger for God. Zacchaeus had heard the stories about Jesus of Nazareth and yearned to see and hear this young prophet for himself. In Zacchaeus's early years, he probably defined happiness as getting what he wanted. But over time he realized true happiness comes from wanting what you get. Ultimate poverty is being so poor that all you have left in life is money.

But [he] could not because of the crowd

Sometimes it's the people who surround Jesus that make it more difficult to clearly see Him. I read that Mahatma Gandhi had once wanted to know Jesus in a personal way. After returning to South Africa from his studies in England, he began a law practice. Gandhi wanted to know God better and tried to attend a church service, but an usher refused to give him a seat because of the color of his skin and told him never to return. Gandhi, like Zacchaeus, desired to see Jesus, but he was not allowed by the crowd surrounding Him.

Stanley Jones, a missionary, once asked Gandhi why he was so against becoming a Christian though he often quoted Christ. Gandhi responded, "Oh, I don't reject Christ. I love Christ. It's just that so many of you Christians are so unlike Christ."[1] Although Gandhi was a great man, he was not able to see past the crowd to Jesus.

For he was of short stature.

Zacchaeus's real problem was not with Jesus or even the crowd surrounding Jesus; the problem was his own height. He was an unusually short man, and this made it difficult for him to see over the people. The real problem is seldom the barriers people place in our way but rather the ease with which we let them become our excuse. Zacchaeus may have been physically short, but this did not diminish the stature of his spirit.

So he ran ahead

Obstacles did not discourage Zacchaeus; he was too experienced for this. He understood that wherever he found people, he would find problems. So he did not let the people who surrounded Jesus turn him off or turn him away.

This is the decision that set Zacchaeus apart: he refused to turn from Jesus just because some people were in his way. We don't always get what we want, and we seldom receive all we deserve. The things we do obtain and hold onto are the things we value enough to go after and fight for.

To reach Zacchaeus's rank in the tax collecting business required a certain level of ingenuity, intelligence, and grit. This little man's career had hinged on his ability to overcome the unwillingness of his subjects to pay. He obviously learned to do these things very well to have become the "chief tax collector."

During my years of ministry, I have noticed something strange. People can be very capable when it comes to the affairs of this world, but they often lose their nerve when it comes to the things of God. Zacchaeus, however, did not.

Zacchaeus didn't waste a moment in self-pity. He did what any executive is expected to do. He recognized a problem and formed a strategy to solve it. Chuck Swindoll, a great teacher, observed that life is 10 percent what happens to you and 90 percent how your respond.[2] We are seldom limited by what we cannot do as much as by what we will not do.

And [he] climbed up

Zacchaeus did not let his pride get in his way. He was willing to use whatever resources were available to rise above his personal limitations and get a glimpse of Jesus. If we are on a path with no obstacles, it's probably because the path is not leading anywhere special.[3]

Let's be honest. The real reason we give up our pursuit of God is seldom the difficulties we face but the fact that we just don't want it enough. This man, however, was willing to do whatever it took to rise above the crowd around him for a clear view of the man who had the power to change his life.

Into a sycamore tree to see Him

Sycamore trees have low, spreading branches and can grow to be very tall. This tree in Jericho was a godsend for this little man. Sometimes a person can actually "walk up" a sycamore. Some sycamores have trunks wide enough for climbers to wrap their legs around and inch up until they can grab a branch. If the latter was true of Zacchaeus's tree, he may have gotten a little scraped and bruised as he climbed up, but the thought of seeing Jesus was worth it. Whatever it cost to get to the other side of his limitations, he was willing to pay.

For He was going to pass that way.

If you knew where Jesus was going, what would you be willing to sacrifice to get there? Some of us won't even drive a few minutes in an air-conditioned car to a place with padded seats to be in God's presence.

You may have heard the saying, "Opportunity is missed by most people because it is dressed in overalls and looks like work." Zacchaeus may have missed God every other day of his life, but he was determined not to let it happen on this day!

And when Jesus came to the place

A quarterback does not throw the ball to where the receiver is; he throws the ball to where the receiver is heading. If God's blessing is not where you are, it is because you are not yet where you need to be going.

The Roman philosopher Seneca reportedly commented, "Luck is what happens when preparation and opportunity meet."[4] Some in the Jericho crowd probably dismissed Zacchaeus's good fortune as luck. But we notice that the harder he tried, the "luckier" he became. What critics consider luck is really God's blessing on people who are willing to take God-shaped risks and follow their hunger.

He looked up and saw him

In season, sycamore trees would be full of leaves and fruit. I can imagine this despised man trying to camouflage himself behind the foliage to stay safe from a hostile crowd while he waited for the moment to catch a glimpse of Jesus. Instead, Jesus saw him first.

Zacchaeus was not a perfect man. He was probably not even a good man, but he had the wisdom to seek Jesus. People may try to overlook, block, or discredit such a person, but the promise remains that God "is a rewarder of those who diligently seek Him" (Hebrews 11:6). God's rewards and benefits are always beyond anything we can hope for or imagine. All this tax collector wanted was a glimpse of Jesus, but God, in characteristic form, exceeded his wildest dreams.

And [He] said to him, "Zacchaeus, make haste and come down, for today I must stay at your house."

In this traditional culture, a person only took the liberty of inviting himself to the home of someone with whom he was very close, that is, a longtime friend or a relative. The familiarity used in this invitation was Jesus' way of embracing Zacchaeus. It was like the pope giving a mafia figure a shout-out and telling everyone that he was going to spend the evening with that family.

Jesus was willing to expose Himself to ridicule for associating with perhaps one of the most notorious characters in that society. Of all the people Jesus could have stopped to spend the evening with, He chose this sinful man. If Jesus was willing to stop and spend time with someone as nefarious as Zacchaeus, why would He not stop for me or for you?

So he made haste and came down, and received Him joyfully.

According to the Jewish historian Josephus, a militant group known as the Zealots actively but surreptitiously assassinated Roman collaborators in the first century. It was not unusual for a person like Zacchaeus to be covertly dispatched while in a busy crowd. And we know a certain Zealot named Simon was one of the twelve disciples. Surely his friends were in the crowd (Matthew 10:4 ESV).

Considering the potential danger of the situation, Zacchaeus sat in the tree and hoped no one would notice him. Jesus, however, not only noticed him but spoke to him and called him down. Jesus obviously loved the tax collector as much as He did the Zealot, just as He loves the Democrat as much as the Republican and the rich as much as the poor.

This reminded me of a civil rights roundtable I attended on Capitol Hill with my boss, who was a civil rights leader at the time. Some of the greatest social justice warriors of the eighties were there. About twenty minutes into the meeting, a woman and her aide entered the room from behind me. I didn't see who it was, but I noticed people start to whisper. She sat down in the chair right next to me. I looked over and recognized Coretta Scott King.

I expected someone to ask me to move to another seat, because I most certainly was in the wrong place. After a few minutes, no one said anything to me about moving. So to avoid being rude, I mustered the courage to introduce myself to Mrs. King. She looked at me and smiled.

It was an amazing experience to be that close to an iconic, history-changing figure. Mrs. King comported herself perfectly. I watched her mannerisms close up, listened to her responses, sat on the same platform, and even shared the same air with her. It was one of the bigger "pinch me I must be dreaming" moments in my life. Surely Zacchaeus felt this way when Jesus said He would be coming to visit him in his home.

But when they saw it, they all complained, saying, "He has gone to be a guest with a man who is a sinner."

The grace of God is the most outrageous truth in all of the universe. It confounds the self-righteous, alarms the proud, angers the powerful, but it is the only hope for any of us. Some ask the question, why would a good God hang out with bad people? The unfortunate answer is that this is the only type of people there are. All of us fall short.

The apostle Paul said that it's this kindness that leads us to repentance (Romans 2:4). Why? Because kindness creates gratitude. Gratitude creates loyalty. Loyalty to a holy God gradually woos us away from every sin (Titus 2:11–12). If the tender compassion, kindness, and long-suffering of a loving and self-sacrificing almighty Being does not soften a hardened heart, nothing else can.

Then Zacchaeus stood and said to the Lord, "Look, Lord, I give half of my goods to the poor."

Notice Zacchaeus did not say half his salary; he said half of all he owned. When a greedy tax collector, without any pressure, starts giving away half his money to the poor, you know something awesome has happened. Most religions teach that God will love us more when we do better. Jesus, on the other hand, loves us at our worst and, only then, teaches us that we can do so much better (Romans 5:8).

"And if I have taken anything from anyone by false accusation, I restore fourfold."

The Mosaic law required people to compensate those they had defrauded by returning what was taken plus 20 percent. Zacchaeus offered those he had harmed 400 percent! His repentance was not demonstrated in words alone but in deeds. When the grace of God truly impacts our lives, our willingness to make restitution will not only abound but overflow.

Just one encounter with Jesus was enough to show this despicable man that true greatness is not measured in what we have but by what we give. I believe Zacchaeus was able to sleep better than he had in years after his heart became right with God. There is no pillow as soft or sleeping pill more powerful than a clear conscience.

And Jesus said to him, "Today salvation has come to this house, because he also is a son of Abraham."

People could question Jesus' methods, but they could not question His results. Zacchaeus was public enemy number one, as bad as any man could be, but the presence of Jesus in his home caused a change no one could deny.

In the second clause, Jesus reinstated this once conniving traitor back into the Jewish community by calling him a son of Abraham, the father of the Jewish people. God's discipline is always designed to be redemptive.

When Jesus called Zacchaeus a son of Abraham, He was re-establishing the tax collector as a brother to everyone in the family of God. We can choose our friends, but we cannot choose our family.[5] This statement was as controversial as anything Jesus could have said on that day.

"For the Son of Man has come to seek and to save that which was lost."

This statement is a summary of Jesus' mission and also a rebuke to the Pharisees, Sadducees, and scribes who alienated the lost instead of trying to reach them. They did not understand that all are in some way lost; it's just that some people's lostness is a little more obvious.

Despite Zacchaeus's many flaws, he was willing to recognize a spiritual opportunity, make the necessary transitions, and when his chance arrived, he seized it with all his heart. This little man's heartfelt hunger caused him to not only receive a bird's-eye view of Jesus, it resulted in a life-changing evening with the true king of Israel.

My Story

Like Zacchaeus, I learned how a few moments in the presence of Jesus can change a life forever. When I was in the tenth grade, my parents were concerned I might not graduate high school. After yet another let down, my dad was fed up and took me for an angry walk at the park around the corner with the hill. I imagine God was looking down from that hill, thinking, *There goes that boy again.*

My father told me I had better find a way to graduate high school and then enlist in the army. Maybe that would make a man out of me. Using colorful language he knew would get my attention, he let me know in no uncertain terms that I had better stop breaking my mother's heart.

I didn't realize the impact I was having on my family, but my dad's words were the reverse psychology I needed. When I realized the best he thought I could do was graduate high school, I took it as a challenge and quickly turned my grades around. I took an SAT class and somehow did well enough to be accepted into Howard University in Washington, DC.

During the school year I worked after school, but the summer after I completed high school, my work schedule was irregular and I had a little more free time. I began to read for enjoyment for the first time. Reading opened an entirely new world to me.

Among the first books I read was *The Autobiography of Malcolm X*. In those pages I met a man angrier than I was. His in-your-face fearlessness captured my imagination.

Malcolm X dared to call Christianity the white man's religion, and from my vantage point I could only agree. After all, it was Christians who went to church on Sundays but kidnapped, shipped, enslaved, and raped my great-great-grandparents. I agreed with Malcom that the turn-the-other-cheek approach to living in America made African Americans docile and weak. Why should we remain nonviolent while our enemies practiced the worst kind of institutional and physical violence?

In elementary school my first fight was with a white kid who called me the N-word; my first rejection came when a little white girl told me her dad would not permit her to walk home with my group of kids because we were black. On and on. I was a child of the seventies and integration was new, but I took these events quite personally.

Stories of my family members reinforced my animus. I watched television shows with people who looked like me being bitten by police dogs, knocked down by high-pressure streams of water screaming from fire hoses, and beaten and clubbed for trying to cross the color barrier in the South. It made me angry that this was the legacy of my so-called Christian country.

My family had a strong sense of racial pride. My dad was part of the March on Washington in 1963, a member of the NAACP, and a leader in the Democratic Black Caucus in Long Island. My mother told me the only time she had ever seen my dad cry was when Martin Luther King Jr. was assassinated in 1968. I had tremendous respect for Dr. King, but I felt his greatest philosophical impediment was his Christianity. I could not comprehend the logic of letting someone beat me in order for them to eventually accept me. On the other hand, Malcolm X reportedly said, "Sometimes you have to pick the gun up, to put the gun down." That kind of reasoning I could understand.

It was true that African Americans were outnumbered and armed resistance was unlikely to succeed, but my thinking was we could raise enough hell that we might eventually be kicked out to build our own independent nation. When I entered college that fall, my ideas were quickly reinforced by members of the Nation of Islam who stood outside the student center and delivered weekly sermons. They were impressive, and it seemed everyone was intimidated by them.

Louis Farrakhan and others from the reorganized Nation of Islam visited the university frequently. I began to read the *Final Call* newspaper and some of Elijah Muhammad's books. I must admit I was quickly disappointed by the lack of depth, but I could sympathize with his passion.

By the beginning of my sophomore year, I decided to stop listening to secondary voices about what Malcom called the black man's true religion. I read the Quran from cover to cover. I was surprised to find Jesus mentioned. Later, I even read much of the encyclopedic Hadith. As I read, I discovered that Islam was at least as oppressive to African culture as the Europeans ever were. But as I entered my early years of college, I was becoming more and more convinced that Islam was the only viable religion for persons of color.

During these early college years I gradually began to come out of my shell. I was still a relatively quiet guy, except when arguing a point in class or debating with friends over a few beers. This was an exciting season in my life.

I had a lot of friends. My grades were pretty good. I always had a job that kept some money in my pocket. But what I enjoyed most was engaging the million new ideas that were swirling around in my head. Life was good!

Then one day in my second year, I experienced something I could not explain. There was nothing in my background that provided a frame of reference for understanding this experience. All I knew was that I suddenly began to feel emotionally and spiritually naked and very self-conscious. I felt a tangible sense of lostness, and none of what I felt made any sense to me. Nevertheless, it was as real as the chair in which I sat. I tried to ignore it, but it only grew more intense.

I could not shake this feeling. I thought maybe I was experiencing some type of mental breakdown. Maybe I had been reading too much and studying too hard. So after the class was over, I put on my poker face and headed back to my downtown dorm to work this thing out privately and pull myself together.

The fifteen-minute bus ride felt like an hour. When I finally reached my apartment building, I got off the bus and went up the elevator. When I arrived at my apartment, I was relieved to find none of my roommates there. I thought, maybe if I just lie down for a little while, I could shake what I was feeling and get back to normal.

As I stretched out across my bed, it was like my guts where trying to tell me something that they didn't have adequate English words to explain. I had such a deep consciousness of being off course, I slid from the bed to the floor. While sitting there, I felt trapped from going forward by some type of a barrier. I could not explain my feelings.

This sensation was horrible but somehow familiar. Before this moment my heart only spoke in whispers, just below the noise of life. But this was like someone had turned up the volume of my deepest feelings. I always knew I was a mess, but I found ways to drown it out with other things. While I sat on the floor, I could not hide from it. I was completely flustered by my inability to solve this existential crisis. Then, out of nowhere, I saw the image of a man in a robe. And all He said was three words: *This is it.* As if to say His Presence is what I had been looking for so intensely in all the wrong places and faces for so long.

I felt the same Presence I had felt at summer camp as a child. Immediately I knew it was Jesus.

I could not believe what I was experiencing. I jumped up and looked in the other bedroom to see if someone was playing a trick on me. I opened the front door to make sure I had not overheard anyone speaking in the hall. I came back into the apartment and ran into the bathroom, looking behind the curtain to check the shower. I was struggling to find a natural reason for what I could not explain. Everywhere I looked was empty.

God had obviously remembered the sixteen-year-old who stood atop the ridge in the park and shook his fist at heaven and demanded that God reveal Himself. As powerful as this moment was, I was still not interested in becoming a Christian. Sophocles once said, "Stubbornness and stupidity are twins." I did, however, begin an intense study of the Gospels. I was not ready to go to church, but I stopped reading the Quran. My reading of the Quran had been purely intellectual, but as I read the Gospels, somehow Jesus leaped out of the pages and began to come alive to me. He was so different than I had imagined or heard explained. He was the most interesting and compelling personality I had ever studied.

However, I had a major hurdle it would take me a year to overcome. I refused to read the parts of the Gospels that described His crucifixion. It was an absurdity to me. Why would a man as powerful as Jesus allow Himself to become the victim of such a humiliating death? The cross just did not make sense.

In the Gospels we meet a Jesus who walked on water. There were moments when His face shone brighter than the sun. He subdued gale-force winds with just His words. He defied physics by multiplying matter with the fishes and loaves. He opened blind eyes, healed the sick, and cast out demons and all manner of insanity. He walked through angry, often violent, crowds without being harmed. He taught as no man before Him. Yet the Gospels said He let himself bleed and die (Matthew 14:22–33; 17:2, Mark 4:35–41, John 6:8–11, Matthew 4:24, Luke 4:29, John 7:46).

Eventually it would dawn on me that only a loving almighty God could resist the temptation of self-preservation. The highest use of power is not its exertion over the elements, demons, and other human beings; it is the power we exercise over ourselves for others. Jesus did not do what other men would have done in His circumstances because He was so much more than just a man. Over time the very thing I could not accept became the thing that made me believe.

Mohammad's body is said to be entombed in Medina. Jesus' tomb is empty. Mohammad conquered the Islamic world by killing, but Jesus conquered hearts with His own death. Mohammad asked forgiveness for sins; Jesus lived above sin and died for the sins of others (Surah Ghafir 40:55, John 8:46, 2 Corinthians 5:21). The differences go on and on. People who say that Mohammad and Jesus are the same know very little about either.

Jesus' unique courage and His willingness to sacrifice for

others gradually gripped my heart. I began to feel both a freedom and indebtedness that is hard to describe. Helen Keller observed, "The most beautiful things in the world cannot be seen or touched—they must be felt by the heart."[6]

The prophet Isaiah summed up the cross hundreds of years before it happened: "Surely He has borne *our* griefs and carried *our* sorrows" (Isaiah 53:4, emphasis added). Jesus bore all that we cannot bear and carried all that we could not carry. The cross is about God coming to earth to pay a debt He did not owe because we owed a debt we could not pay. "Yet we esteemed Him stricken, smitten by God, and afflicted."

Alone and without the support of anyone on earth, He took not only our griefs and sorrows but did it while people like me criticized Him. I can't think of a greater display of strength than for a man to do this. It would be just a short period of time before the greatest miracle in human history—the resurrection—would change my life. The resurrection is the final proof to us that the worst thing does not have to be the last thing.[7]

Summary

- Some define success as getting what you want, but true happiness comes from wanting what you get.
- Instead of making an excuse, make an effort.
- Life is 10 percent what happens to you and 90 percent how you respond.
- We are seldom limited by what we *cannot* do and mostly by what we *will not* do.
- The favor of God is drawn to those who are in the right spot.

Self-Analysis

1. Is there an area in your life where you stopped instead of passing through to a greater destiny? Have you found yourself settling for what is comfortable rather than what is best?
2. When have you recently blamed another person or something else for your own shortcomings?
3. When was the last time you went out on a limb for God?
4. Can God trust you to be where He wants you to be when He wants you to be there?
5. Has the Holy Spirit made you aware of a step of faith you need to take today? Ask the Lord to help you go out on a limb for Him.

THREE

THE MAN GOD LOOKED FOR

After this there was a feast of the Jews, and Jesus went up to Jerusalem. Now there is in Jerusalem by the Sheep Gate a pool, which is called in Hebrew, Bethesda, having five porches. In these lay a great multitude of sick people, blind, lame, paralyzed, waiting for the moving of the water. For an angel went down at a certain time into the pool and stirred up the water; then whoever stepped in first, after the stirring of the water, was made well of whatever disease he had. Now a certain man was there who had an infirmity thirty-eight years. When Jesus saw him lying there, and knew that he already had been in that condition a long time, He said to him, "Do you want to be made well?"

The sick man answered Him, "Sir, I have no man to put me into the pool when the water is stirred up; but while I am coming, another steps down before me."

Jesus said to him, "Rise, take up your bed and walk." And immediately the man was made well, took up his bed, and walked.

And that day was the Sabbath. The Jews therefore said to him who was cured, "It is the Sabbath; it is not lawful for you to carry your bed."

He answered them, "He who made me well said to me, 'Take up your bed and walk.'"

Then they asked him, "Who is the Man who said to you, 'Take up your bed and walk'?"

But the one who was healed did not know who it was, for Jesus had withdrawn, a multitude being in that place. Afterward Jesus found him in the temple, and said to him, "See, you have been made well. Sin no more, lest a worse thing come upon you."

The man departed and told the Jews that it was Jesus who had made him well.

(JOHN 5:1–15)

In the late 1970s the *Superman* movie became a phenomenon. With groundbreaking special effects and a fresh Clark Kent played by Christopher Reeve, it became a blockbuster. The movie was nominated for several Academy Awards and was followed by multiple sequels throughout the 1980s.

In 1995 the actor who had become best known as the Man of Steel fell from his horse and broke his neck. He became a quadriplegic and remained so until he died in 2004. The pain and suffering caused by this injury is almost inconceivable to those with the freedom of mobility. Yet he told *Esquire* magazine, "Some people are walking around with full use of their bodies and they're more paralyzed than I am."[1] It appears the worst type of paralysis is not the kind that happens to a body but the kind that happens to a heart. Oswald Chambers said, "The great paralysis of our heart is unbelief."[2]

In this chapter we will learn about a man's decision that liberated him from both inward and outward paralysis. After thirty-eight years of suffering, he was able to break his cycle of impotence and become not only a person Jesus stopped for but also someone Jesus looked for.

After this there was a feast of the Jews, and Jesus went up to Jerusalem.

All male Jews were required to travel to Jerusalem to attend three mandatory feasts (Exodus 23:14). This may surprise some people, but

God enjoyed celebrations even in the old covenant. Each festival was a commemoration of what God had done in the past and, by implication, what He would continue to do for His people in the present and in the future.

Jesus did not come to abolish the law but to fulfill it (Matthew 5:17). So it should not be surprising that Jesus participated in all the Jewish festivals, even the feasts that were not binding. Though He was famously guilty of breaking the burdensome, unreasonable human traditions added to the law, He remained passionate and fully observant to the law until His death (Matthew 23:4–21; Mark 7:9–13).

Now there is in Jerusalem by the Sheep Gate

According to Nehemiah, the Sheep Gate was within the eastern wall.[3] Through this gate sheep were herded to be sacrificed in the temple. As Jesus journeyed with His people through this gate, little did they know that they were traveling with the actual Lamb of God, the embodiment of everything the Jewish law had pointed to for nearly fifteen hundred years. This Lamb who would die to save us was also the Shepherd who was to lead us.

A pool, which is called in Hebrew, Bethesda, having five porches.

Bethesda literally means "house of mercy," and the spring that fed the reservoir was thought to have healing powers. Eventually five roofs were built over the pool and were later used to protect the multitudes from the sun and rain. The roof structure loosely resembled pavilions similar to picnic areas today. But believe me, the conditions were anything but a picnic!

In these lay a great multitude of sick people, blind, lame, paralyzed

Desperate people made pilgrimages to the pool from all over the land and hoped to receive a miracle. The sick, blind, lame, and paralyzed packed every inch of the area. Due to medical advances today, it is hard for us to grasp the amount of sickness and suffering that gathered around this pool. But clustered along the water's edge were the worst and most hopeless of all medical cases in this region of the world.

People with broken, bruised, and often infected body parts migrated to this pool, which measured about three-fourths of a city block. The sight was both horrifying and heartbreaking. Without occasional breezes, the smell was suffocating.

Waiting for the moving of the water.

Some scholars suggest an intermittent spring gushed into the pool area, causing the water to foam and bubble. Others say the next verse was an editor's note mistakenly copied into the text to explain a superstition to later readers. I am not exactly sure what stirred the water, and it is not essential that we know. What is clear is that people believed healings happened to those who entered the water whenever it was moved.

> **For an angel went down at a certain time into the pool and stirred up the water; then whoever stepped in first, after the stirring of the water, was made well of whatever disease he had.**

This was a dog-eat-dog, zero-sum environment. The only person who succeeded was the person who entered the water first; everyone else lost. These five colonnades were filled with people who faced failure 99.9 percent of the time.

The pool was surrounded by chronic losers, people unable to contribute to their families or society. If they had not been completely abandoned, they became a drain on everyone who loved them and traveled to care for them. All of us have felt or will feel at some time and in some way a little like these desperate people.

The good news is that of all the places Jesus could have been in Judea that day, He chose to stop here, with people who no longer measured up and people who didn't have the strength to do the things they wanted to do. Since God's personality never changes, He will do the same for us today.

> **Now a certain man was there who had an infirmity thirty-eight years.**

Out of the crowd, Jesus singled out a "certain man." Nothing was recorded in the gospel to explain who he was or why he was alone. But something unusual about this man is mentioned: he had been suffering with an illness longer than the average lifespan of the time.

The man experienced longevity without a remedy, and such a blessing at times feels more like a curse. I think the only reason this man had survived so long was because God was not yet finished with him. Every day your head is above ground is proof that God is not yet through with you either.

When Jesus saw him lying there, and knew that he already had been in that condition a long time

This is why Jesus was so different: He "saw him." He really saw people. He didn't just see the man's problem, He saw the man. This is also what is scary about Jesus. He doesn't see what you would like Him to see but rather who you really are and what you really need.

About thirty years ago I heard a story on the radio. Unfortunately, I can't remember who told the story, but it was powerful. One day a boy found a multicolored caterpillar. Its colors, wiggly body, and numerous legs fascinated him. He gently picked it up and took it home. At home the boy placed it in a box. He added a stick for it to climb and brought leaves for the caterpillar to eat. Every day he studied the caterpillar and built a strong bond with it.

Eventually the caterpillar began to build a cocoon. The boy was excited, knowing the caterpillar would soon turn into a butterfly. He checked on his pet several times a day but became concerned the caterpillar was taking too long to emerge from its cocoon.

Finally, about a week into the process, something happened. A small hole appeared in the cocoon, and the boy expected the butterfly to quickly surface. But as he watched, his pet seemed to struggle to break free from the shell. The boy was disappointed there was very little progress.

Hours passed. The butterfly was working its hardest, but it just could not break out. Heartbroken at the sight of this struggle, the boy decided to help.

With a pair of scissors the boy cut a small opening in the cocoon to make it easier for the butterfly to emerge. Almost immediately the butterfly exited without any more struggling. But when it appeared, the boy was surprised. Instead of being the beautiful butterfly he anticipated it would be, it was grotesque. It had a swollen body and short, shriveled wings.

He watched the butterfly over the next few days, hoping the wings would dry out, enlarge, and expand. But that never happened. The butterfly crawled around with its withered wings and huge body for the rest of its life. It never flew and soon died.

The boy was heartbroken and told his mom about the dead, misshapen butterfly. His mother took him to a science teacher to find out what had happened.

The teacher taught the boy a very important life lesson. He explained it was essential for the butterfly to struggle out of its cocoon. As it pressed its way through the tiny opening, the pressure would force excess fluids out of its body and into its wings. It was this struggle that allowed butterflies to fly.

This is the reason God intends for us almost always to play a role in His miracles. It's not that God can't do wonders without us, it's just, if He did, we would never get a chance to grow. Your struggle today, as hard as it may be, is God's helping you to develop the strength He knows you will need tomorrow.

He said to him, "Do you want to be made well?"

Notice the question: "Do you want to be made well?" Jesus did not start with the problem on the outside of the man, He started with the one on the inside—his "want to." The problem was not just the man's useless legs but the immobility of his heart. The man had lost something far more valuable than the ability to walk, namely, the willingness to hope.

When we endure painful situations for a long time, it's easy to become so accustomed to the pain that we gradually accept it as our new normal. When this happens, victims become as much a part of their problem as the actual disease or circumstance.

The famous football coach Vince Lombardi observed, "Winning isn't everything—but wanting to win is."4 The loss of a game may show for a few minutes on a scoreboard, but the loss of heart will show up for life.

The sick man answered Him, "Sir, I have no man to put me into the pool when the water is stirred up."

When we don't like a question, we tend to change the subject. That's what this man did. Instead of answering the question—whether he wanted to be made well—he talked about his lack of support. This was certainly a deflection, but it belies the deeper reality that loneliness can be as hurtful as physical pain.

The wealthy could hire others to carry them into the water. But this man had no servants, no friends, and thus no options. I am sure someone tried to help him at some point, but if you are down too long, people have a way of moving on with their lives.

"But while I am coming, another steps down before me."

The man just could not compete. A little friendly competition is good and can cause us to excel. It's amazing how I am able to jog so much faster and longer whenever I run with a friend. Healthy competition brings out the best in us. But to create a competition between the sick, blind, lame, and paralyzed is cruel.

Every time the water moved, everyone looked out only for themselves. People increased their odds by pushing others out of their way. Every time the spring bubbled, this man was reminded how alone he was and how much of a failure he had become. It was only a matter of time before his circumstances impacted his heart.

The story is told that through a storefront window a boy watched a man getting a tattoo. He was able to read the words "Born" and "To" inscribed on the man's arm. The boy was excited about what would come next—until he saw the final word was "Lose." He asked his grandfather why a person would tattoo such a self-defeating statement on his forearm. The grandfather replied, "It was tattooed on his heart long before you saw it on his arm."

Jesus said to him, "Rise"

After nearly forty years in this condition, this man could not have been more helpless. This is important to grasp if you are going to understand the way God generally performs miracles. Jesus would not heal this man's body without the man exerting himself. As Frederick Douglass observed, "Opportunity is important but exertion is indispensable."[5] Our greatest successes always begin with a decision to try.

In summary, Jesus told the man to do what he could not do. The delicate balance between God's sovereignty and the use of this man's free will is in play here. An everyday illustration of interdependence may help. The average adult can run about ten to fifteen miles per hour. The fastest man in the world, however, can run almost twice that speed. But if you put a person behind the wheel of a Formula One race car, that driver can easily travel at more than two hundred miles an hour. Although the car does all the work, the driver must at least press the gas pedal and steer the car. It is the combined efforts of the driver and the car that make such high-speed travel possible. It is our cooperation with God that helps us win the day.

"Take up your bed and walk."

Jesus told the paralytic to carry the thing that had supported him for so many years. His transformation was so radical that he first had to carry off the proof of his old condition for anyone to believe him. His thirty-eight-year-old tearstained sheets were about to become a badge of honor. God wants to turn your bed of affliction today into a symbol and trophy of His grace tomorrow.

And immediately the man was made well, took up his bed, and walked.

As radical as the demand Jesus put on this man, God only moved as the man dared to obey. The Greek dramatist and playwright Aeschylus said, "Obedience is the mother of success and is wedded to safety."[6] The safest choice we can ever make is to obey the one who holds the universe in the palm of His hand! When He says move, move, and when He says stop, stop; it's not rocket science.

Notice, the paralyzed man was healed without stepping into the water. Jesus is greater than any healing angel, paralyzing demon, or anything superstition can muster. When Jesus became involved, this man no longer had to compete with his neighbors for healing. We don't have to be the fastest, strongest, or most popular; we only need to be obedient and willing to receive.

> ### And that day was the Sabbath. The Jews therefore said to him who was cured, "It is the Sabbath; it is not lawful for you to carry your bed."

The Mishnah, also known as the Oral Torah, states in *The Talmud of the Land of Israel*, "A man could not transport an object from one place to another on the Sabbath," along with thirty-nine additional commandments the Jewish fathers added to the original law of God. Every observant Jew knew these requirements by heart and followed them. If not, they would face the wrath of their religious authorities.

Instead of the authorities being excited about this man's healing, they focused on the fact that he was not acting according to these regulations they added to God's Word. The prophets had prophesied for centuries that the deaf would hear and the blind would see when the Messiah came (Isaiah 35:5). Instead of rejoicing that Jesus had fulfilled the credentials of the long-awaited Messiah, they fussed that He did not abide by certain rules of their particular denomination. Human laws can be helpful and even wise safeguards; however, if they clash with God's written Word, we must always choose to obey God rather than men (Acts 5:29).

> ### He answered them, "He who made me well said to me, 'Take up your bed and walk.'"

I imagine a little attitude in this man's tone. I think the conversation in his head may have gone something like this: *All these years that I was sick, you Pharisees, scribes, and Sadducees did nothing to help me get well. You offered no help for thirty-eight years. Now, all of a sudden, you think I owe you an answer? It was not your regulations that healed me, but the guy you think defied them! Who do you think I should give greater credence to?*

Like spoiled children, the learned leaders completely overlooked this man's remarkable improvement in his quality of life and focused on the trivialities instead. I would have thought, *This Jesus may not have attended the same school you guys did or been accepted into the same country clubs, but He did something you evidently could not. I think I would do better to listen to Him.*

Then they asked him, "Who is the Man who said to you, 'Take up your bed and walk'?"

"Who is the man?" or as some translations say, "Who is this fellow?" These religious rulers were furious. Confronting controlling people is never fun. They are threatened by anyone who sees things a little differently and does not do exactly as they say. If God had intended for people to live under this much control, we would all have been born with a remote control attached to our chests.

But the one who was healed did not know who it was

The paralyzed man was so focused on his own situation and healing that he neglected to get to know the one who made it all possible. God's miracles are not only designed to help us but to draw us closer to Him. Still, millions confuse occasional answered prayer with knowing

God. As the old adage reminds us, even a blind squirrel finds a nut every now and then.

We've all heard, "Give a man a fish and you feed him for a day. Teach a man to fish and you feed him for a lifetime." Likewise, "Give a man a miracle and you will bless him for the day. Teach a man to know the God behind the miracle, and the blessing will last a lifetime."

For Jesus had withdrawn, a multitude being in that place.

It is safe to assume that when this miracle happened, not only did the healed man get excited, but the people around him also saw what had happened. Keep in mind these were the people who wrestled, pushed, and shoved each other to get into the stirred water before anyone else. Jesus did not want the people who trampled one another to get to the water to get hurt trying to reach Him, so He had to withdraw. Jesus had to leave the conversation unfinished in order to protect others.

Afterward Jesus found him in the temple, and said to him, "See, you have been made well."

The use of the word *found* implies a search. Jesus had a "leave no man behind" policy two millennia before the US Marines. He refused to leave His encounter with this once physically paralyzed man incomplete (Philippians 1:6). The paralytic's body was healed, but Jesus was concerned with the far deeper issues that had obviously contributed to the man's condition.

"Sin no more"

Jesus had freed the paralytic from an effect of sin but not the cause. It's not that there is always a one-to-one relationship between sin and sickness, but in this case there clearly was.

Researchers today suggest the way we think in our hearts can seriously affect our health and healing. Studies show that long-term guilt and shame have a physiological impact. Many mental health experts try to help people manage these emotions by eradicating the concept of sin, but Jesus was not that naïve about the human condition or the laws of the universe.

Jesus never intended to change the moral law as communicated by Moses. He just offers forgiveness when we fall short and gives a new grace-empowered heart to do better. Jesus would not ask us to do something He did not first make possible for us to do. The moment Jesus spoke the words, "Sin no more," God released all the power this man would ever need to be free from the area in which he was struggling. As C. H. Spurgeon noted, "When we deal seriously with our sins, God will deal gently with us."[7]

"Lest a worse thing come upon you."

The most astonishing part of this conversation was the former paralytic's staggering alternative. Jesus believed there was something worse than being paralyzed for thirty-eight years. He thought there was something worse than living in squalor and having no one to help. Denying the existence of hell may make us feel more at ease, but it will not lower its temperature even by one degree (Revelation 14:11; Mark 9:44).

As much as Jesus loves each of us, He would never lower God's standards to accommodate a follower's unwillingness to raise his or hers. If we do not allow God to raise the bar, how will we ever learn how high we can soar?

The man departed and told the Jews that it was Jesus who had made him well.

Jesus explained eternal life elsewhere saying, "This is eternal life, that they may know You, the only true God, and Jesus Christ whom You have sent" (John 17:3). Eternal life is not just unending existence but a life of deep personal acquaintance with Jesus. By the time the former paralytic left Jesus, he no longer had any questions about who his healer was.

The once paralyzed man returned and answered the religious leaders' questions. His motives are not clear. Perhaps he was trying to reach them by providing the information they originally sought. Others suggest he turned on Jesus because His demand that he "sin no more" was too high. I do not fully understand this man's response or the nature of his sin, but I would soon begin to understand my own.

My Story

A year had passed after I encountered Jesus in my dorm room. I was in my third year of college. I was continuing to read through the Gospels. I was gripped by the man named Jesus but deeply skeptical and uncertain about church. Amazingly, God knows how to speak every language, and He decided to speak mine.

I asked my buddies about a girl I had met at the end of my sophomore year. We had some chemistry, and I wanted to connect. My buddies told me she attended the noon chapel services held on campus a few times a week. So a buddy and I decided we would attend the services to take a closer look.

My friend had more of a religious background, so he was a lot more comfortable in the worship service than I was. Although this service was on campus, it felt like I was in a completely different world. There were no hymnals open, and the music was not outdated like at camp. Everyone passionately sang songs to Jesus.

The place was electric. It seemed like everyone except my friend and me had their arms lifted toward heaven. Eventually the speaker spoke. I cannot remember what he said, but he had a confidence in his words that did not match his size. It was mesmerizing.

My buddy and I went back a few times, but it didn't take long for me to start attending on my own. Initially I had come to check out a girl, but soon the desire to attend was all my own. The chapel atmosphere always left me hungry for more.

The girl and I quickly became an item. One night in her apartment, while reading Matthew's gospel, a verse captured me. It was as if the words leaped off the page and were being spoken personally to me: "Therefore I say to you, do not worry about your life, what you will eat or what you will drink; nor about your body, what you will put on. Is not life more than food and the body more than clothing?" (Matthew 6:25).

The message went straight to my heart, but my mind could not ignore its implications. I tried to dismiss the experience, so I struck up a conversation with her housemate, who happened to be an ordained minister. God really knows how to set up circumstances. God's secret providence is a greater mystery than even revelation.[8]

We talked for more than an hour. Near the end of our conversation, the minister got a little strange. He said, "You are ready. What are you waiting for?"

I was thinking, *Ready for what?*

The next day I attended the chapel service as normal. When the speaker finished the message, the minister I had talked with the previous night grabbed my arm. I was not used to a guy touching me, so my first instinct was to hit him, but inside I knew he was only trying to help.

Standing up to help me the way he did in a room full of other students took a lot of courage. I walked with him to the altar. I felt self-conscious standing before so many, but somehow I knew the struggle was over. I was deeply grateful someone looked past my hardened façade and helped me break my paralysis, which was more of a paralysis of overanalysis rather than raw fear.

But finally I was willing to surrender to the fact that I might not be 100 percent sure about what I was doing, but if I didn't take the risk, I would never know. After I prayed with one of the leaders, an assurance that is hard to describe came into my heart. I instantly knew I had made the right decision, but I felt a deep foreboding that the road ahead would not be all cookies and ice cream. I had made the most far-reaching decision of my life, and Christianity as presented by Christ is not only hard, it is impossible.

I was still the foulmouthed skinny kid who had learned to hit first and ask questions later. I matured a lot in college and even grew enough to walk away from a few fistfights. I got bored with always arguing my point and became a much more sensitive and caring person. But the life Jesus calls His followers to is daunting.

Like the paralytic by the pool, I wanted to walk, but such steps would require a miracle.

The paralytic who Jesus found near the temple was set free from his physical ailment. But to remain free, he was going to have to deal with a certain touchy subject, namely, his sin. Today, many people sneer at the concept of sin, thinking it is an antiquated concept. But by reading a few posts and blogs, you will find many people are as passionate about modern concepts of right and wrong as any Bible-thumping caricature ever was.

In the Hebrew language the word that is translated as *sin* simply means to "miss the mark," as an archer who shoots and misses the bull's-eye. The reason sin is so tricky is that to be off by only one degree does not appear consequential at first. But as the arrow travels over longer distances, the smallest deviation can result in missing the entire target.

If an arrow is off by only one degree per foot, we will miss our target by two-tenths of an inch in the first foot. After three hundred feet we will miss our target by a little more than five feet. After a mile we will be off by about ninety-two feet. But for every sixty miles the arrow travels, we will miss our target by roughly a mile. The trap is that the chains of sin are too light to be felt until they are too heavy to be broken.[9]

Theologian John R. W. Stott explained, "For the essence of sin is man substituting himself for God (Genesis 3:1–7), while the essence of salvation is God substituting Himself for man (2 Corinthians 5:21). Man asserts himself against God and puts himself where only God deserves to be; God sacrifices Himself for man and puts Himself where only man deserves to be."[10]

This may surprise you, but before God helped me adjust my philandering and racial attitudes, my temper, and the thousand things that were off the mark in my young life, He struck at the root: my tongue.

The greatest freedom we enjoy is not the freedom of movement, assembly, the press, or the right to bear arms but the personal freedom to choose our attitudes and ultimately our words. With this freedom comes our greatest responsibility.

The reason why words are so important is because Jesus teaches us that what comes out of our mouths always gets its start in the heart (Matthew 15:8). The only way to get our mouths right is for us to get our hearts right. Without God's help, the human heart is impossible to tame.

James, the half-brother of Jesus, added, "If anyone does not stumble in word, he is a perfect man, able also to bridle the whole body" (James 3:2). If all our words suddenly materialized, would we be arrested for assassination, murder, theft, assault, robbery, and countless sex offenses? God knew if He could help me regulate my speech, everything else would begin to follow. Like the paralytic Jesus found in the temple, if I continued to think too lightly of sin, I would eventually think too lightly of my Savior.[11]

Summary

- People often confuse experiences with God with following Him.
- Even when confronting lifelong problems, it is never too late with God.
- The first step to breaking your paralysis is listening to Jesus but then standing up for yourself.

- God helps people who want to change, grow, and improve their lives.
- Jesus came not only to forgive us of our sins but to *free* us from our sins.

Self-Analysis

1. What are two things you have waited so long for that you have now given up on ever receiving?
2. How has frustration or disappointment paralyzed you?
3. If God followed up on the good things He has done for you, what would He say?
4. Have you followed the instructions God has given you? In what area of your life do you need further instruction? What is your plan to get it?

FOUR

WHEN GOD STOPPED BY

On the third day there was a wedding in Cana of Galilee, and the mother of Jesus was there. Now both Jesus and His disciples were invited to the wedding. And when they ran out of wine, the mother of Jesus said to Him, "They have no wine."

Jesus said to her, "Woman, what does your concern have to do with Me? My hour has not yet come."

His mother said to the servants, "Whatever He says to you, do it."

Now there were set there six waterpots of stone, according to the manner of purification of the Jews, containing twenty or thirty gallons apiece. Jesus said to them, "Fill the waterpots with water." And they filled them up to the brim. And He said to them, "Draw some out now, and take it to the master of the feast." And they took it. When the master of the feast had tasted the water that was made wine, and did not know where it came from (but the servants who had drawn the water knew), the master of the feast called the bridegroom.

And he said to him, "Every man at the beginning sets out the good wine, and when the guests have well drunk, then the inferior. You have kept the good wine until now!"

(JOHN 2:1–10)

It was Wednesday, August 28, 1963. It was supposed to be a three-hour program called the March on Washington for Jobs and Freedom. The final speech of the day was to be given by thirty-four-year-old Martin Luther King Jr.

He was on the heels of the Birmingham campaign. Birmingham was one of the most dangerous and racially divided cities in the country. Dr. King had just completed his seminal *Letter from Birmingham Jail,* which he started by writing on the margins of a newspaper given to him by a janitor. He eventually finished it on a legal pad his attorneys were allowed to leave for him.

Today he has a national holiday in his honor that almost all celebrate, but back then Dr. King received both praise and criticism from the African American community as well as the national press. He was nearing the height of his career, and there was tremendous pressure on Dr. King to succeed as never before. He and Clarence B. Jones had several conversations about the main points of the 1963 speech. Then the moment of truth arrived.

He stood before a quarter of a million people and delivered the first seven paragraphs of the prepared speech. But about twelve minutes into it, he heard Mahalia Jackson, his favorite gospel artist shout, "Tell them about the dream, Martin! Tell them about the dream!" He looked at her and paused.

The two were very close. She had often sung before his speeches, from the time of the Montgomery boycott in the 1950s until the present. Over time they had developed huge mutual admiration and trust for each other, and, thank God, he listened.

After she shouted, he slid his text to one side of the stand. Then he grabbed the lectern and looked at the crowd and spoke from the heart extemporaneously. One of the most meaningful and memorable oratories in history followed because a friend encouraged him to improvise and let the moment carry him.

Prussian and German military strategist Helmuth von Moltke (1858–91) observed, "No battle plan survives contact with the enemy."[1] If we are going to be successful in life, we have to be willing to adapt to setbacks, difficulties, and changing environments. Or as my mother would tell me, "You have to learn to roll with the punches."

In the second chapter of the gospel of John, we read of a similar instance. Jesus and His disciples were invited to a wedding celebration in a nearby town. During the celebration, a surprise shortage arose, and instead of scolding the family for their mismanagement, Jesus improvised, using the limited resources they had, and saved the wedding.

This was Jesus' first recorded miracle in the Gospels, and He would never again get a second chance to make a first impression. This miracle was significant on several levels. First, He performed this miracle not to meet a necessity but a luxury. Perhaps God is not as austere as many believe. Second, this miracle did not save anyone's life or limb but merely rescued a family from embarrassment. Perhaps God cares more about our feelings than we imagine. We are going to discover much more in this story because this miracle offers tremendous insights into the heart of the Man we all need to stop by.

On the third day, there was a wedding in Cana of Galilee

In John's gospel thus far, Jesus had been baptized by John in the Jordan, the Holy Spirit had descended on Him like a dove, and He had been tempted by the Devil for forty days in the wilderness. He then had a remarkable first meeting with Andrew, Simon, Philip, and Nathanael and returned home. Three days later He headed for a wedding just outside His hometown.

Weddings in the Jewish culture were not just family but public celebrations. Entire communities took part and celebrated the union of the new couple. The finest food, wine, and accommodations were provided.

First-century Jewish weddings were very different from those held in the United States today. The formalities often took place after years of preparation, and the final celebration could last up to a week. Even the shortest weddings lasted at least two days.

By this time in Jewish history, the marriage ceremony was conducted with attention to rigorous and methodical detail. There were even specific days on which women could be married: virgins married on Wednesdays and widows on Thursdays. Any departure from established protocols would result in reproach and public shame.

And the mother of Jesus was there.

Mary had probably been ostracized during her pregnancy and after the birth of Jesus, since the first step of a Jewish marriage (signing the Ketubah) is the last step in modern weddings (signing the marriage license). Once the bride's father and the groom signed the document, the couple was for all intents and purposes legally married. The marriage was not physically consummated until the father of the bride allowed the groom to come to his home and begin the sexual relationship with the bride.[2]

When Mary was pregnant without her family's arranging for the first night (*chuppah*),[3] it was a disgrace not only for her but for her family. In this part of the world, memories were very long. Over time she evidently managed to overcome much of the stigma associated with her pregnancy before her chuppah, because we see in this verse she is likely given the honor and coveted role of overseeing the details of a wedding. Some might even say she was the event planner for this wedding.

Now both Jesus and His disciples were invited to the wedding.

The stained-glass image of Jesus as a dour-faced Messiah has little support from Scripture. Since His baptism by John, the redemptive clock had begun ticking. Jesus only had a certain amount of time left on earth, yet He spent nearly a week at this wedding, which tells us marriage is very important to God.

Weddings were happy times. People were not invited to just attend weddings as they are today. A herald visited the homes of the guests and requested they dance and rejoice at an upcoming wedding. So people danced through the streets as they celebrated the couple's marriage. More dancing followed when they reached the main wedding venue.

It was not uncommon for special guests, such as Jesus, to dance individually for the bride and groom.[4] I wonder if Jesus was asked to do His thing. I can imagine the other guests laughing and clapping as they enjoyed His extraordinary rhythm and grace. I would have loved to have watched all this unfold.

And when they ran out of wine

Wine was an important part of a Jewish wedding.[5] Typically, women and children did not drink highly fermented wine. It is not clear whether it was as strong as today's wines. Nonetheless, it certainly had some level of alcohol and played an important social role.[6]

Parents began to dream and prepare for a child's wedding very early. A proper marriage was paramount in the ancient world. Any failure in this regard could stigmatize the marriage and the reputation of the family for years.

At the height of the wedding festivities at Cana, the unthinkable happened. The groom's parents had invited more guests than they could supply with wine. They ran out. Due to rigid social conventions, according to one Bible dictionary, a family could have been sued if there were any lack in the wedding provisions.[7] So this was no small matter, and most families were very careful about ensuring ample provisions were available for all.

In the eleventh verse, John recorded this was the first of the signs performed by Jesus. In the Bible, a miracle is always a supernatural event. The difference between a sign and a miracle is a sign is not always supernatural. Astronomical and geological events were sometimes considered signs. What makes an event signatory is that it points to something profound. So the question is, what did this miracle signify?

The Bible clearly warns against drunkenness and alcohol abuse. Proverbs tells us, "Wine makes you mean, beer makes you quarrelsome—a staggering drunk is not much fun" (20:1 THE MESSAGE). Nonetheless, used properly wine typically represents joy and gladness throughout the Scriptures (Psalm 104:15).

Marriage is one of the most ancient and sacred biblical institutions. The lack of wine at this wedding represented the loss of joy in sacred activities. People were so bogged down observing the letter of the law, they missed the spirit and stopped having fun. Have you ever allowed falsely expanded religious requirements to suck the life out of what would otherwise be an exciting journey?

What is awesome about this narrative is we discover we don't have to hide our unhappiness from Jesus. In fact, He is the first person we should run to whenever we run out of wine and stop having fun.

The mother of Jesus said to Him, "They have no wine."

Since Mary doesn't call Joseph to help her, most scholars conclude he had already passed away, which would mean Jesus can identify with what it is like at some point not to have a father in the house. As a widow and a single mother, the first-century Jewish culture required that Mary look to her oldest son for assistance.

This passage vividly captures why Mary is a model of intercession for so many. When people she cared about were in trouble, she didn't waste time criticizing them. She didn't broadcast their problems to everyone. She took the problem to Jesus. Imagine what might happen if more of us today were like Mary?

It's during our clumsy and ill-prepared moments like these wedding hosts experienced that we discover who our true friends are. Mary understood too well what it was like to feel undeserved shame and embarrassment. She knew what it was like to have people look down on her. She knew what it felt like to be taunted, belittled, and laughed at. She did not want this for her friends in Cana.

Jesus said to her, "Woman, what does your concern have to do with Me?"

If your family is like mine, any conversation that begins with my calling my mother "woman" would not go well. In the Middle East, this was a little more common. It was a polite but firm way for Jesus to create boundaries between His mother and Him. Despite Leonardo da Vinci's frail depictions of the Savior, Jesus was nobody's mama's boy. He made it clear in every possible way He was His own man.

Familiarity and respect seldom come in the same package. So we should not be surprised when the relationship between Jesus and His family became complicated (Mark 3:21). He was Mary's baby boy and big brother to all His siblings, but He was still chiefly their Messiah. He had to create healthy limits to protect His mother and family from crossing the line.

Jesus had outgrown her lap, though she would never outgrow His love (John 19:25–27). Like every other healthy parent-child relationship, Mary had to give Jesus room to make decisions on His own. A good parent must know when it is time to let go. It takes courage to release our children, but it's our letting go at the right time that often helps us keep them close in the long run.

"My hour has not yet come."

Every time Jesus talked about His hour in the gospel of John, He was referring to His death on the cross. Here He was saying, "Mama, if I answer your request the way you want me to, it's going to send me to an early grave." Sometimes people trying to influence us just don't know what they don't know.

Jesus knew the more public His miracles became, the more resistance and controversy He would stir up and the closer He would be to the cross. He had years of preaching and teaching to offer, and He wanted to fly under the radar as long as possible before He created the circumstances for the inevitable.

His mother said to the servants, "Whatever He says to you, do it."

Jesus had just straightened out His mother. Notice she did not respond by rolling her eyes. She was humble enough to make the adjustment. Not only did she submit to what Jesus said, she asked everyone around her to do the same.

The key to a long-term relationship with Jesus is very simple: No matter who you are, or who you think you are, just find out what Jesus says and do it! Jesus is either Lord of all or Lord of none. His life leaves no middle ground. C. S. Lewis observed:

> I am trying here to prevent anyone saying the really foolish thing that people often say about him: I'm ready to accept Jesus as a great moral teacher, but I don't accept his claim to be God. That is the one thing we must not say. A man who was merely a man and said the sort of things Jesus said would not be a great moral teacher. He would either be a lunatic—on the level with the man who says he is a poached egg—or else he would be the Devil of Hell. You must make your choice. Either this man was, and is, the Son of God, or else a madman or something worse. You can shut him up for a fool, you can spit at him and kill him as a demon or you can fall at his feet and call him Lord and God, but let us not come with any

patronizing nonsense about his being a great human teacher. He has not left that open to us. He did not intend to.[8]

> Now there were set there six waterpots of stone, according to the manner of purification of the Jews, containing twenty or thirty gallons apiece.

These stone water pots were used for religious ritual washings. Many authorities tell us this water was used for ritual immersion. The use of this water symbolized washing away from the body the spiritual grime of life and represented cleansing from all physical defilement. This water had been earmarked for external use. Jesus, however, had in mind an internal purpose.

> Jesus said to them, "Fill the waterpots with water." And they filled them up to the brim.

They needed wine but only had water, more than a hundred gallons of it. Have you ever had a whole lot of one thing and you were grateful for it, but it didn't make up for the thing that was missing?

Maybe you are a good provider but not so good at being a father. Maybe you have more than enough vision but not enough money. Maybe you are a great friend but not so much a lover. Jesus is about to show us how to deal with the missing ingredients in our lives.

His first step was to use what they had: water pots. If you wait until God gives you what you want before you use what you have, you will never get to where you are going. God blesses those who are willing to make the most of what they have, not what they wish for.

Jesus instructed the servants to completely fill up the pots with water. They had to first fill the pots because God wants us to understand that our obedience and not our resources ultimately makes the difference. What they were willing to do by faith, filling the water pots, qualified them for the wine. Faith always requires a corresponding action.

And He said to them, "Draw some out now, and take it to the master of the feast."

The host knew they were out of wine. You may not realize this, but wine is roughly 90 percent water. So they already had most of what they needed. Yet only after they brought what they had to Jesus did He supply them with what was missing.

God is not angry about what you lack. He is not upset with what you are missing or the places you come up short. He just asks that you trust Him and give Him what you have and take whatever steps He gives you and let Him make the difference. Whenever I bring Jesus what I have, He always turns it into something it has never been and could never be without Him. It's just what He does.

And they took it.

We do not know if the miracle happened while the water was in the pots, when they drew the water out of the pots, or as they took it to the master of the feast. The point is, after they obeyed, the miracle happened. Heartfelt obedience is an ultimate channel of spiritual power. I don't know exactly when God is going to show up in your situation.

All I know is that if you obey Him with what you have, He will at some point make it happen.

During the Civil War, Abraham Lincoln met with a group of ministers. One of them said, "Mr. President, let us pray that God is on our side." The president responded with great wisdom: "No, gentlemen, let us pray that we are on God's side."⁹ God is only responsible for the consequences of our obedience.

When the master of the feast had tasted the water that was made wine, and did not know where it came from (but the servants who had drawn the water knew)

This is my experience every time I talk about Jesus on Sundays. I prepare all weekend to fill my water pots before I speak. But I am not always sure if the water has turned to wine in the preparation or if it will happen in the sharing. All I know is that I must do both. At some point, as I obey, God will add whatever is missing and bridge whatever is needed to somehow add value for those who hear.

The master of the feast called the bridegroom. And he said to him, "Every man at the beginning sets out the good wine, and when the guests have well drunk, then the inferior."

It was typical that, as the evening progressed and people became more and more tipsy, the quality of the wine could decline. The more people drank, the duller their senses became, and the less taste mattered. The master of the feast recognized the wine Jesus had created tasted better than the wine previously served.

Jesus' transformation of the water into wine was a sign point-ing out the *New* Testament would be far more enjoyable than the *Old* Testament. Conventional wisdom led one to serve the best wine first and then the lesser vintage, but Jesus was not a conventional Messiah.

"You have kept the good wine until now!"

The Devil tends to give us his best first. Drug addicts are forever try-ing to recapture that elusive first high and often kill themselves trying to do so. Adventurers try to relive the thrill of their first exploit, so they keep outdoing themselves and pushing the envelope until tragedy strikes. God is the opposite. Like a great bottle of wine, His plan only gets better with time.

God designed the inaugural sign performed by Jesus to illustrate an eternal principle: God always saves the best for last. No matter how great or how difficult your life is, if you walk with Jesus, it will only get better. A good working definition of heaven is that those going there understand their best days are always ahead. A good working definition of hell is that those going there know their best days are behind them. There is much truth in the old adage, "True happiness is simple: someone to love, something to do, and something to look forward to."[10]

At this wedding, Jesus was willing to go off script. He had some reluctance, "My hour has not yet come," but He was willing to improvise by taking what they had and turning it into something they could never have without Him. The great American composer George Gershwin observed, "Life is a lot like jazz . . . it's best when you improvise."[11]

My Story

As the nation celebrated the first observance of Dr. King's birth-day, a Washington, DC, disc jockey made a comment that angered many people in the nation's capital. He remarked that if the assassination of one African American leader would result in a holiday, we should shoot four more and get the whole week off.

When I heard this, I delivered an impromptu speech at the student center and helped to lead several days of protests in front of the radio station. Hundreds of students came together, and the disc jockey was eventually suspended. Later in the 1990s this man was fired for playing an excerpt from a Grammy-nominated R&B song and saying, "No wonder they drag them behind trucks," referring to the 1998 murder of James Byrd, an African American, in Texas by a white supremacist. It angered me that such a popular voice in the DC community would take the violent death of African Americans so lightly.

Our protest at the radio station was successful and meaning-ful, but as I was willing to call out others, I had to be willing to also challenge people in my own community. There was no question in my mind whether the student protest was right, but I had led the protest alongside several black Muslim leaders, and after meeting with the station owners, some things were said about the Jewish station owners in private that were as intolerable to me as the disc jockey's statement about Dr. King.

There was a time I would have discounted such com-ments, but something had begun to change in my heart. In the past, I thought if white people did not want my family in their neighborhoods, stores, restaurants, or schools, why should I care what they think. Instead of wasting time trying to change other people's minds, I'd rather use that energy to build my own neighborhood, stores, restaurants, and schools. I began to realize my black nationalism not only did not jibe with the spirit of reconciliation pervasive in the life of Jesus, but it also created a new set of moral problems.

I intentionally attended a historically African American university because it had mostly African American students and professors. All my friends were African Americans. In my teenage years, I dated only African American girls. In my free time, I only read books by African American authors and even worked a job where only African Americans were on payroll. We all cope with painful realities in different ways. My response to racism was not so much to fight it but to find ways to better avoid it.

In the 1970s, both my New Jersey and Long Island neighborhoods were not so welcoming to the blacks who were moving in. In middle school, black and white students jeered each other on the bus. The high school had race riots. They were "them" and we were "us," and from a practical standpoint I didn't care if it ever changed.

What was amazing about Jesus is that, though He was a Jew, He talked with Samaritans. Though He was a man, He engaged women (John 4). Though He was the Son of God, He spent His days talking with people. The distinctives that we often make so important rarely seemed to have fazed Him in the least.

The skin color of Jesus is not clear in the Bible. There were light-skinned as well as dark-skinned Jews. Instead of taking sides in ethnic arguments, He superseded them by His plan to give birth to a completely new race of people taken from every race or people group. Jesus said, "Most assuredly, I say to you, unless one is born again, he cannot see the kingdom of God" (John 3:3).

The kingdom of God is simply men and women who have been spiritually born into a new race, a new family, with God Himself as our Father. The dividing line in the kingdom Jesus taught about was not white versus black but spiritual light versus spiritual darkness.

Rabbi Abraham Joshua Heschel made this penetrating observation: "Racism is man's gravest threat to man—the maximum of hatred for the minimum reason."[12] I decided that if I were going to truly be a follower of Jesus, I had to make some adjustments in my mind-set and fully explore these new truths and find a way to live them out. I challenged myself like never before. Though Washington, DC, was full of good African American churches at that time, I decided to attend an interracial church in Maryland that was led by an Italian pastor.

The drive was about forty minutes. It required gas and extra drive time that was hard on a student budget and work schedule. But I felt it was necessary for me to get my heart right. I was nervous and skeptical, but over time I began to embrace people of different races. I found that though we may look a little different and have different cultural advantages, we are all the same. I realized the ultimate solution to prejudice and bigotry lies within the heart and ultimately the message of Jesus Christ and not in a new nation.

Studies show that roughly 65 percent of people who identify as Christians are not active in any church.[13] If just a small percentage of these people would do as I did as a young man and regularly attend biblically sound churches that are led by a person of another ethnicity, I am convinced the racial division in the churches of America would go a long way toward healing. Congregational leaders would be less comfortable holding unexamined and misinformed attitudes that negatively affect a significant part of their congregations. Also, it is more difficult to make blanket statements that might hurt people who are your close friends.

The first Sunday I attended the Maryland church, the pastor's message focused on the passage in which Jesus restored Peter after he had betrayed Him (John 21:15–19). I didn't understand why it resonated so deeply within me, but I knew I was in the right place. A few weeks later, while visiting a girlfriend and her roommate, we began to talk about God and our experience at this new church. As we were talking, I heard someone say, "If you love Me, feed My sheep." I asked them if they heard the voice. They rolled their eyes as if I were teasing.

Both these young ladies had been Christians much longer than me. I could not imagine why I heard something they did not. This was the first time since my sophomore year in the dorm that I had heard that voice with such intensity. I left the apartment to walk in the night air to try to make sense of what had just happened.

I reflected on my pastor's message, how Peter went back to his fishing trade after he denied Jesus. He even took the other disciples with him, and as they fished Jesus watched from the distant shore.

As was often the case in the Gospels, they had not caught any fish and were probably frustrated. So Jesus shouted to the disciples to cast their net on the right side of the boat. As soon as they did, fish filled their nets. Instantly, Peter realized that voice had to have been Jesus' because He had done the same thing once before (Luke 5:6).

When he realized it was Jesus, Peter jumped out of the boat

and swam to shore while the others pulled in the net with all the fish. When he got to shore, three times Jesus asked Peter if he loved Him, each time in slightly different ways. This was the same number of times Peter had denied knowing Him in the high priest's courtyard:

> So when they had eaten breakfast, Jesus said to Simon Peter, "Simon, son of Jonah, do you love Me more than these?"
>
> He said to Him, "Yes, Lord; You know that I love You."
>
> He said to him, "Feed My lambs." (John 21:15)

Each time Peter responded affirmatively, and Jesus responded by asking him to be a shepherd or pastor his flock instead of going back to his natural and family trade.

From childhood, my dream was to one day be like my father. He was a businessman and worked in corporate America. I wanted to do the same.

I knew that God spoke these words that evening to tell me He wanted me to let go of my business aspirations for full-time service in His kingdom. While a student, I not only worked various jobs but ran my own business. My résumé was pretty strong for a guy whose dad thought he might not graduate high school, and everything on my horizon seemed bright. I had to choose between my plans and improvising.

Seven paragraphs and twelve minutes into Dr. King's great "I Have a Dream" speech, he found the courage to choose between his notes or his dream. That night, I couldn't imagine how this impatient, ill-tempered, unstable, unsteady introvert could ever be of any use to God.

Dr. King said the following two months before his death:

Everybody can be great, because everybody can serve. You don't
have to have a college degree to serve. You don't have to make
your subject and your verb agree to serve. You don't have to
know about Plato and Aristotle to serve. You don't have to know
Einstein's theory of relativity to serve. You don't have to know the
second theory of thermodynamics in physics to serve. You only
need a heart full of grace, a soul generated by love.[14]

I didn't think I had the temperament and certainly not the
character, maturity, or level of spirituality expected of a pastor,
but I could not shake what I knew the Lord was saying to me. I
continued to attend the weekly noon meetings on campus at the
Rankin Chapel. I also attended the weekly prayer meetings in the
basement of the chapel. My thinking was that although I may not
be ready to lead, I could learn to serve.

At the nightly meetings I found myself naturally talking more
and more about my faith. Then one night I caught myself preaching to the small group. I was surprised, but the chaplain kept
nodding. So I continued. He noticed what was taking place and
allowed me to share regularly in the evening meetings.

By the fall semester I began preaching the noon service at
Rankin Chapel twice a week. I had come full circle and became
a leading speaker in the ministry where I first gave my life to the
Lord. The ministry began to grow from a handful of students to
hundreds. It was not because my messages were so good, but
that I was so passionate about the life-transforming power of
Jesus.

It was an exciting time, but it put a terrible strain on my natural
disposition. I barely slept the night before I spoke. I would perspire
through my shirts and sometimes shake all day until the speaking

engagement was over. I felt under attack by my own fight or flight instincts. My stomach did flip-flops and couldn't keep down food. Waves of self-doubt flooded my mind. My internal conflict was as bruising as any fist fight, but I had to find a way to maintain my composure because I was not going to let Derek Grier go out like that. I fought so hard internally that one time I passed out in front of two hundred students.

I preached that Jesus brought peace, but I only had that peace while I preached. Before I stood I felt I wanted to roll up into a ball. And after I taught I never felt I had said things quite right. It was harder than anything else I had ever done. If doing anything else in life would have pleased God, I would have done it in a heartbeat.

Public speaking was like having a really bad dream over and over again that I couldn't wake up from. I prayed daily that God would allow me to do something else with my life. Surely I was not naturally suited for this role.

The words of Charles Hadden Spurgeon, one of the greatest preachers of all time, gave some sobering advice: if one can do anything else besides ministry and be happy, then do it.

> I have met ten, twenty, a hundred brethren, who have pleaded that they were sure, quite sure that they were called to the ministry— they were quite certain of it, because they had failed in every- thing else. . . . "The ministry needs the very best of men, and not those who cannot do anything else." A man who would succeed as a preacher would probably do right well either as a grocer, or a lawyer, or anything else. A really valuable minister would have excelled at anything. There is scarcely anything impossible to a man who can keep a congregation together for years, and be the

means of edifying them for hundreds of consecutive Sabbaths; he must be possessed of some abilities, and be by no means a fool or ne'er-do-well. Jesus Christ deserves the best men to preach his cross, and not the empty-headed and the shiftless. . . .

We must try whether we can endure brow-beating, weariness, slander, jeering, hardship; and whether we can be made the off-scouring of all things, and be treated as nothing for Christ's sake. If we can endure all these, we have some of those points which indicate the possession of the rare qualities which should meet in a true servant of the Lord Jesus Christ.[15]

I was certainly not what Spurgeon called the best of men, but I soon learned to embrace the browbeating, weariness, slander, and jeering that better men learned to handle. But the same mouth I was trying so hard to give to the Lord was the very thing that once yielded would set in motion some of the most soul-seeking and harrowing days of my life.

Summary

- Before God does the impossible, He waits until it is impossible.
- Whatever Jesus says for you to do, *just do it.*
- God often asks us to work with what we have before He gives us what we want.
- Sometimes it feels like God is taking too long to help you. But there is a reason.
- Sometimes you have most of what you need; you just need God to add a few missing ingredients.

Self-Analysis

1. The last time your closest friend had a problem, did you just point out the problem, or did you roll up your sleeves to help solve the problem?
2. Do you sometimes confuse "not yet" with "no" when it comes to God's timing?
3. When push comes to shove, is God's Word or your general experience your greater guide?
4. What are the top two missing ingredients in your life: love, patience, humility, hope, or something else?
5. What is it you sense God is calling you to do today?

FIVE

GOD STOPPED TO GET IN

Immediately Jesus made His disciples get into the boat and go before Him to the other side, while He sent the multitudes away. And when He had sent the multitudes away, He went up on the mountain by Himself to pray. Now when evening came, He was alone there. But the boat was now in the middle of the sea, tossed by the waves, for the wind was contrary.

Now in the fourth watch of the night Jesus went to them, walking on the sea. And when the disciples saw Him walking on the sea, they were troubled, saying, "It is a ghost!" And they cried out for fear.

But immediately Jesus spoke to them, saying, "Be of good cheer! It is I; do not be afraid."

And Peter answered Him and said, "Lord, if it is You, command me to come to You on the water."

So He said, "Come." And when Peter had come down out of the boat, he walked on the water to go to Jesus. But when he saw that the wind was boisterous, he was afraid; and beginning to sink he cried out, saying, "Lord, save me!"

And immediately Jesus stretched out His hand and caught him, and said to him, "O you of little faith, why did you doubt?" And when they got into the boat, the wind ceased.
(MATTHEW 14:22–32)

I n the 2010 movie *Catfish*, Vince told Nev, the lead character, a folksy story:

> They used to tank cod from Alaska all the way to China. They'd keep them in vats in the ship. By the time the codfish reached China, the flesh was mush and tasteless. So this guy came up with the idea that if you put these cods in these big vats, put some catfish in with them and the catfish will keep the cod agile. And there are those people who are catfish in life. And they keep you on your toes. They keep you guessing, they keep you thinking, they keep you fresh. And I thank God for the catfish because we would be droll, boring and dull if we didn't have somebody nipping at our fin.[1]

In life, we are either in the middle of a storm, heading into a storm, or heading out of one.[2] Sometimes God leads us into adversity not because we are weak but to keep us sharp and strong. We all need the rain, but like the disciples, we would prefer it rained without bad weather.

Immediately Jesus made His disciples get into the boat

Jesus had just finished feeding the five thousand, and the Bible said that Jesus had "made" or obligated His disciples to take this journey. The majority of these men lived around this sea all their lives. Peter, Andrew, James, and John were fisherman who daily fished these waters. These fishermen knew this sea like the backs of their hands. Intuitively, they felt in their bones a storm was brewing.

Their reluctance about getting into the boat was understandable. One of the most amazing things about this narrative is that despite their misgivings, apprehensions, and fears, they were willing to trust the carpenter from Nazareth and get into the boat anyway.

Compounding the fear of an ensuing storm was the fact that Jesus had earned a tremendous amount of confidence from the disciples. They were hesitant to leave the peace and security they found at the side of their Teacher. And yet Jesus intentionally sent them into an oncoming tempest. Surprisingly, this was not a mistake but a part of His plan. A ship is safest in the harbor, but that's not what it is built for.[3]

Good teachers will faithfully invest hours instructing their students and then test their students to prove what they have learned. Whenever we can't hear God's voice during a trial, remember "the teacher is always quiet during the test."[4]

And go before Him to the other side

Jesus provided His disciples with unambiguous instructions. He didn't say for them to go into the middle and sink. He told them to go to the other side and He would meet them there. All of us have a place called "the other side" that requires overcoming obstacles to reach. Everything of value in life is always on the other side of fear.[5]

While He sent the multitudes away.

Jesus needed some private time with the Father. Jesus was not like most of us. He didn't try to find time to pray, He made time to pray. The demands of life often conspire the hardest against a quality prayer life. Satan tries so hard to limit our praying, only because he knows our prayers will limit him.[6]

The disciples got in the boat. Jesus stayed behind to pray for their courage. Few things prove our love for people more than heartfelt and continued prayer. Jesus had thousands of people and their needs pressing on Him, but He sent the crowd away. The key to a successful prayer life is a willingness to dismiss anything that attempts to crowd out God. The disciples were heading into a storm, so Jesus headed to His knees. Here are a few things God promises about prayer:

The prayer of a righteous person is powerful and effective. (James 5:16 NIV)

This is the confidence we have in approaching God: that if we ask anything according to his will, he hears us. (1 John 5:14 NIV)

Therefore I tell you, whatever you ask in prayer, believe that you have received it, and it will be yours. (Mark 11:24 ESV)

If you remain in me and my words remain in you, ask whatever you wish, and it will be done for you. (John 15:7 NIV)

And when He had sent the multitudes away, He went up on the mountain by Himself to pray. Now when evening came, He was alone there.

Jesus went up the mountain alone to pray. He lived in constant contact and company with His disciples, but there were still some things

He could only do alone with the Father. The stronger our private relationship with God is, the greater an asset we can become to our larger community.

I wonder if as He prayed He occasionally looked over the mountain to check on the disciples. Everything Jesus did on earth was with you, me, and all His followers in mind. He saw the sky darken. He felt the wind blowing against His robe but wanted the best for His disciples and understood that "courage is like a muscle, it is only strengthened by use."[7] The disciples were going to need to be strong when He finished His mission and returned to heaven. He had to make sure they were properly conditioned and made battle ready while He was still here.

But the boat was now in the middle of the sea, tossed by the waves, for the wind was contrary.

Storms were very sudden and dangerous on the Sea of Galilee. The sea varies from six hundred to seven hundred feet below sea level. It was surrounded by cliffs to the east, some reaching two thousand feet. Tropical air from the sea often collided with the cooler air from the mountains, which funneled strong, violent weather onto the sea. If you were unfortunate enough to get caught on the water during one of these storms, you were in for one of the most terrifying experiences of your life.

Jesus was alone, praying atop a mountain. He knew the disciples were in trouble. Yet He chose to remain on the mountain rather than help. Sometimes we help people too quickly; after all, a smooth sea never makes a sailor skillful.[8] Our greatest strength does not come from lifting weights; it comes from lifting ourselves up when we are down.[9]

The gospel of John tells us the disciples were about three and a half miles into their journey, thus they had passed the point of no return. They could not go back. They could only go forward. Here is what we need to understand: God would not have led them into this storm if He hadn't given them what it took to get through the storm. I am learning that whatever is over my head is still under His feet.

Now in the fourth watch of the night, Jesus went to them, walking on the sea.

The disciples had left Jesus just before sunset. Yet this scripture informs us that Jesus did not appear to them until the fourth watch, which was between the hours of 3:00 and 6:00 a.m. In fair weather, it took less than two hours to sail across this sea. If we calculate the time between sunset and the fourth watch, the disciples struggled in a storm that lasted for at least nine hours.

The wind had blown them off course and off schedule. But remember, Jesus had told them to take this trip. I want to repeat myself: the fact you are struggling does not necessarily mean you are out of God's will. The poet John Petit-Senn observed, "True courage is like a kite; a contrary wind raises it higher."[10] Jesus was doing more than equipping these men with His message; He was arming them with their own testimonies. Nothing builds confidence more than experience.

Jesus waited until daybreak before He went out to the disciples. Their arms probably felt like limp noodles, exhausted from rowing all night against the wind. My guess is most men were trying to row while a couple were bucketing the water out of the boat.

These men felt impotent and abandoned. In their zero hour, all the miracles they had witnessed, all the thought-provoking stories

Jesus had told them didn't seem to help. They were in a life-and-death struggle, and this storm was getting dangerously close to sinking them.

When my wife was pregnant with our first son, we were in a storm much like these disciples. She took a standard prenatal, maternal serum alpha-fetoprotein test in her second trimester. After the test, the doctor called us in for a special appointment. She told us the test indicated our son had a major congenital disease.

We went home and googled spina bifida and were horrified by the images we saw. The possibility our child could be born in a vegetative state and could die within his first few years was overwhelming. The doctor as well as some friends recommended we terminate the pregnancy.

When we refused, the doctor suggested my wife have an amniocentesis. When we arrived to have the procedure done, we were told of its risks. My wife was too far along to guarantee the safe execution of the procedure. We were told that if the baby moved, he could be impaled or, worse, spontaneously miscarry. We were not willing to take the chance.

We canceled the procedure and went home. I prayed but felt nothing. Yet I somehow believed God led us into this situation, and in my heart I believed we would safely get to the other side and our child would be all right. Of course, as the mother carrying the child, my wife felt this even more deeply than I did. I tried to reassure her. "Everything will be just fine," I would say. But sometimes I wasn't sure if I really had faith or was in denial.

During the remaining months my wife underwent numerous special examinations and monthly ultrasounds. While I lay in bed at night, images of worst-case scenarios passed through my mind. I would get up and go into our closet to pray. I would sing worship songs out loud to drown out the noise of my doubts. Sometimes it took hours to quiet my mind. If I stayed at it, eventually peace would come, and I could go back to sleep.

My wife eventually went into labor. After three days the baby began to crown. As soon as this happened, a special signal was sent, and several doctors entered the room. A special table was assembled behind a medical curtain.

Due to the alert status assigned my son, they did not allow me to cut the umbilical cord, which I had expected to do. Instead, they quickly whisked the baby away and placed him on the table behind the curtain. Adrenalin filled my body. I was told to stay put, but I followed the doctors behind the curtain. As I peeked in to see what was happening, the doctors ignored me.

After a few minutes that felt like hours, the tension in the room began to lift. They invited me to come closer and meet my son. They showed me his perfectly formed spine. I raced to my wife's bed to whisper in her ear, "Our son has ten fingers, ten toes, and everything is just fine." We were relieved beyond words!

When you come out of a storm, you are never the same person who entered it. That's what the storm is all about.[11] Sometimes God saves us *from* things (as he did my family), and at other times He keeps us *despite* things, but in either case—Jesus saves!

Mark 6:48 adds some additional information about the story of the disciples in the storm: "Then He saw them straining at rowing, for the wind was against them. Now about the fourth watch of the night He came to them, walking on the sea, and would have passed them by." Here Jesus "would have passed them by." He might not have saved them had they not invited Him to do so. God sometimes shows up without an invitation, but it's important to understand He will not stay without one. I could not make God help me during those restless nights, but I could invite Him in. He not only showed up but has stayed with my wife and family ever since.

My oldest son is now in his twenties, about to graduate college, and is as strong and smart as any other young man his age. God is not a respecter of persons. He can do for you what He has done for us!

And when the disciples saw Him walking on the sea

God was trying to show the disciples the deepest part of the ocean is barely a puddle to Him. David, the shepherd and king, wrote, "If I say, 'Surely the darkness shall fall on me,' even the night shall be light about me; indeed, the darkness shall not hide from You, but the night shines as the day; the darkness and the light are both alike to You" (Psalm 139:11–12). There is no dark place in our lives that is beyond His reach or care. Sometimes the intensity of our crisis is calculated to reveal to us the magnitude of our Savior.

They were troubled, saying, "It is a ghost!" And they cried out for fear.

Someone scarier than the storm appeared to be walking on the sea. The hair on the back of the disciples' necks stood up. Their blood pressure spiked, and stress hormones went into overload. They were terrified!

Imagine you were in a storm. It was supposed to be just you and your friends present, but a human form appeared and moved closer and closer to you. Whenever God does something for the first time in your life, it can be scary. Many talk about having a relationship with a Jesus that is far too tame to be the same Christ from the Scripture. It's impossible to look off the side of a mountain for the first time and not feel a sense of wonder at its height. We can't look at the deep blue ocean and not be amazed by its strength, depth, and span. Likewise, we can't experience how big Jesus is and not sometimes feel a little afraid.

But immediately

Jesus waited until the fourth watch of the night before He came to the disciples. He may not come when you want Him, but He is always right on time (Job 42:12)! God often waits until we are at our wit's end before He does His greatest works. Maybe He has to wait until we get to the end of all our self-effort and strength because this is the only way we won't take the credit when He turns it around.

Jesus spoke to them, saying, "Be of good cheer!"

Jesus did not feel sorry for them, and He did not want them to feel sorry for themselves. He smacked them in their faces with His response. He told each of them to check their attitude. Until we learn to rejoice in the middle of it, we are not going to come out of it. The Bible tells us, "Count it all joy when you fall into various trials" (James 1:2). In other words, if we don't change our attitudes in the situations, God has no obligation to change our situations.

Jesus was as tough as nails, and He expected His disciples to be the same way. Someone quipped, "A bad attitude is like a flat tire. If you don't change it, you'll never go anywhere." Most of the time we are only as happy as we make up our minds to be.[12]

"It is I; do not be afraid."

Jesus did not ask the disciples to do twenty things. He didn't ask them to do fifteen things, ten things, or even three things. He simply gave them *one* command: "Do not be afraid." If God sends you into a storm, it could only be because He has already given you what you need to get through it. So don't fear!

God will not allow life to demand something from you that He has not put enough in you to handle (1 Corinthians 10:13). The Great "I Am" is with us and our only responsibility is to trust Him. When we do, we will discover He is infinitely greater than any problem we ever encounter.

And Peter answered Him and said, "Lord, if it is You"

Peter had only one question: "Lord, is it You?" He did not require Jesus to explain Himself or to prove Himself. He only wanted Jesus to identify Himself. Once we establish it is God instructing us in a given situation, all the important questions have already been answered.

"Command me to come to You on the water."

Moses didn't need a boat to cross the Red Sea, only a rod. Abraham didn't need to be young to have a baby, only a promise from God. Gideon didn't need thirty-two thousand soldiers to defeat the Midianite army, only three hundred faithful men. We don't need half of what we think we need to be successful in life. And all we need to do is trust and obey.

The disciples were traumatized because their boat was sinking, but God never intended for them to put all their confidence in the boat.

He wanted them to put their trust in His word that told them to meet Jesus on the other side of the lake. If we are not careful, we will start putting our faith more in a particular resource than in our ultimate source: God.

Peter was strong, but even he could not row hard enough to get them across the sea. John was perhaps the smartest, but even he could not devise a plan to reach the other shore. All twelve men's ability together could not defeat this storm. Jesus was about to teach them, when we can't, *God can*!

So He said, "Come."

"The grass withers, the flower fades, but the word of our God stands forever" (Isaiah 40:8). When your life is down to just you and God's Word, you have finally struck something more precious than gold. You can finally get rid of all earthly limitations and live a life bigger than you can ever imagine.

And when Peter had come down out of the boat

You will not get very far staying in the same boat as everybody else. Historian Carter G. Woodson noted, "If you can control a man's thinking you do not have to worry about his action. When you determine what a man shall think you do not have to concern yourself about what he will do."[13] In other words, what you choose to believe will determine how far you go.

We can't change what is true, but when we embrace it, it will certainly change us. Because Peter was willing to trust God's word, he became the only man in sacred history, other than Jesus, to walk on water. Again, you will never do anything great by staying in the same boat of doubt and unbelief with everyone else.

He walked on the water to go to Jesus.

Peter stepped out of the boat and began walking, not on the water, but on the word of Jesus. This word alone provided a sufficient platform for Peter to begin to stand above what would drown anyone else. As the hymnist wrote, "On Christ, the solid Rock, I stand; all other ground is sinking sand."[14]

Peter was doing great until he tried to get logical about an illogical situation. If we are not careful, we can think ourselves right out of our miracle. The Devil understands too well that he can't stop us if we remain focused on God's Word. So he conjures up everything he can to distract us.

Peter was fine as long as his focus was on Jesus. And we will be fine as long as we keep our focus. Think of a gun sight. It's beneficial as long as it is aimed at an attacking bear, but it becomes dreadful if we set it accidentally on a loved one. The power of faith is released in the direction we are looking, whether for evil or for good. At its root, most fear is simply perverted faith. It's the conviction that something bad will happen, instead of something good.

But when he saw that the wind was boisterous, he was afraid

This is a great example of how we let the irrelevant defeat us. What did the wind and waves have to do with walking on water? Did Peter believe he might have walked better on the water if it had been a windless day? Like us, he allowed his emotions to overpower his judgment. And this error could have cost him his life.

And beginning to sink he cried out, saying, "Lord, save me!"

When he began to concentrate on the problems surrounding him, he began to sink. It's one thing to be aware of problems and another to make them our focus. It's one thing to have trouble and quite another for trouble to have you.

When you think about this, Jesus had already saved Peter from the storm, and at this point he no longer needed to be saved from the storm, *he needed to be saved from himself.* The human imagination is so creative and powerful that, if we are not careful, it can create problems that do not really exist. If you can identify with Peter, take a moment and say with him, "Lord, save me!" May the Lord help us to stay out of our own way!

And immediately Jesus stretched out His hand and caught him

People often criticize Peter for sinking into the sea. At least he got out of the boat! An inescapable part of learning to walk is falling down. Toddlers begin on their knees. Then they build up their leg muscles enough to support the weight of their bodies and begin to pull up on things in order to stand. Finally, the child has a burst of inspiration. She gets up and waddles or runs with her feet wide and arms stretched like an airplane, but invariably, if she's not caught, she will fall.

Peter was finally doing what he had never done before. But as he let himself get distracted he began to sink, but he was still smart enough to call on Jesus. And Jesus reached out and caught him. Notice that Jesus didn't abandon Peter because he was sinking, and God will never leave you if you fall, as long as you are trying.

This was all part of Peter's learning curve. If God only saved people who did everything right, none of us could be saved. A friend once told me, "I'd rather try something and miss than do nothing and achieve it every time."

And said to him, "O you of little faith, why did you doubt?"

What's amazing about this verse is that Jesus was saying a person with only a "little faith" could walk on water. Faith is like nuclear energy; it doesn't have to be large to be powerful. The problem is not the size of our faith but the counterweight of our distracting doubts.

And when they got into the boat, the wind ceased.

Every indication is that after Jesus caught him Peter got back on the water and walked with Him back to the boat. I think if Jesus did something as unusual as carry Peter back to the boat, the Bible would have recorded it.

When Peter called out to Jesus and got his focus off the storm and back onto his Savior, he was given a second chance. In front of all the other disciples, Jesus allowed Peter the dignity of finishing what he started. Sometimes God calms the storm, other times He lets the storm rage and He calms the child.[15]

As soon as Jesus got into the boat, the wind ceased. The length of the storm is often determined by how quickly we learn. The promise God gives us is not based on good weather but the good word He has given us and we place in our heart. As with the anecdotal cod-and-catfish story, opposition is designed to keep us on our toes and help us grow stronger. It's not our haters that harm us as much as our doubts and unfocused minds. And I was about to learn this lesson myself.

My Story

I was preaching regularly, at least two services a week at the campus chapel. I was still not at ease about being behind a pulpit, but the once paralyzing panic attacks were becoming more manageable. At first my greatest challenges came before my speaking engagements but with time shifted to after them. I would second-guess everything I had said and how I had said it. Self-doubt and criticism would grip my mind like a vise. I tried to listen to tapes of my sermons but could not hear the words for the screams of self-condemnation drowning them out in my mind.

At night I would wake up in a cold sweat and rethink any moment I thought I might have misspoken. I reviewed my daily encounters and was never completely satisfied with how I handled my interactions with others. Much of my self-criticism was correct. I probably misspoke, miswrote, and did not handle myself as well as I should have, but this was all part of the growing process. Someone said, "Experience is an expensive lesson but the only way to truly learn something." I had to learn to take the good with the bad and get through the bad stuff in order to get to the good stuff.

I continued to pass Nation of Islam speakers on campus, as in my earlier years, whenever I was around the student center. The speakers continued to poke fun at Christians, calling us "Uncle Toms," "handkerchief heads," and agents of the white man. But with my new understanding of Jesus and the many outrageous inequalities and injustices in Islamic history, there was no way I was going to allow these taunts to go unanswered.

In Philippians 3:2–3, Paul rebuffed Jews who trusted in their cultural and racial background for salvation rather than their faith in God by saying, "Beware of dogs, beware of evil workers, beware of the mutilation! For we are the circumcision, who worship God in the Spirit, rejoice in Christ Jesus, and have no confidence in the flesh." This was exactly what I felt these speakers were doing. They were trusting in their skin color rather than the grace of our loving God.

A few years earlier, when I had heard the disc jockey's comments about Dr. King's birthday celebration, I responded with definitive action. Certainly I should respond to these attacks against the King of kings with even more vigor. So I posted a flyer in response, which read, "Beware of Dogs. Allah is not God and Mohammad is dead." The campus went into an uproar. The university quickly canceled chapel service for the day.

I decided I did not need a chapel and preached my message in the campus yard. It was a matter of principle and I refused to back down.

Unlike the speech I gave in the student center two years earlier, when hundreds of students mobilized, nearly a hundred listened when I preached that day, but only one prayed with me at the end. Some students argued with me and others sneered. Most of the Christians thought I was confrontational and unkind. Perhaps they were right, but I was bothered that whenever Muslims used the same freedom and took the same tone, they were cheered. Was I now less free to speak my mind because I was a Christian?

Shortly after this, a university official sent me a message through a friend and told me I was no longer welcome at the school. They did not formally expel me, but he said I was "persona non grata." At the time I was only a few courses shy of receiving my degree, but I decided there was no way I would reenroll at the end of the semester.

I was baffled by the university's response, considering all the emphasis on free speech in my political science courses. Pastors of some of the largest churches in the city advised their young people against attending my chapel services. The university also hosted seminars to counter the idea there were essential distinctions between Islam and Christianity. Chapel service attendance plummeted to around thirty. I was not only shaken but disillusioned to my core. Why was there a double standard for Christians? Why couldn't Christians stand up like Muslims? Why did Christians walk away because of only one message? Why didn't God do more to protect me? Why did I get into this boat when I knew there would be trouble?

I loved and respected Jesus, but I no longer wanted to be a Christian. I didn't want to be part of a community more concerned about the opinions of the prevailing culture than the principles of Christ. I had no problem with people disagreeing with me. In fact, if a chaplain, pastor, or faculty member pulled me aside to show me where I was wrong, I knew I could learn something. Instead, the ad hominem attacks from my elders in the faith made me question my own.

The buddies who had come to school with me had all graduated and moved out of the city. Meanwhile, I was still in DC, grappling with a ruined reputation, ostracism, and a calling I was having difficulty making sense of. I constantly replayed the stinging things people and the university officials said to me. It felt as if the world had moved on, but I was sinking into a black hole. I sank into a three-and-a-half-year depression. I couldn't shake the past. Despite it all, I nevertheless loved Jesus and studied about Him night and day.

I worked odd jobs and spent most of my spare money on books. I prayed several hours every day until both knees were calloused. The only time I felt a reprieve from my depression was when I was learning new things from the Bible. This was not just an intellectual pursuit but my passion; I felt I would either begin to understand God better or I would die trying. The more I studied, the more convinced I became that "the Bible is not man's word about God, but God's word about man."[16] In its pages was my only hope of not only finding God but finding myself.

I continued to write articles for various university newspapers and wrote a few short booklets, but I no longer preached at the university. My Italian pastor had moved to another city. So, I started attending services elsewhere, and I went back to an African American church, but soon my new pastor got into moral trouble, and I stopped attending. I had no one to turn to. Girls stopped dating me. My family wondered about me. And old friends chuckled at me.

The Bible became my only refuge. In it I discovered Joseph, Moses, David, Nehemiah, Daniel, and others. They were all people in much worse situations than my own, but they hung in there and made it. Maybe I would too.

What helped me most was reading about one of my favorites— Jeremiah. He got so mixed up, he said many things I only thought.

So I thought if a man as great as Jeremiah can reach such depths of despair, I must have hope:

> Cursed be the day in which I was born!
> Let the day not be blessed in which my mother bore me!
> Let the man be cursed
> Who brought news to my father, saying,
> "A male child has been born to you!"
> Making him very glad.
> And let that man be like the cities
> Which the LORD overthrew, and did not relent;
> Let him hear the cry in the morning
> And the shouting at noon,
> Because he did not kill me from the womb,
> That my mother might have been my grave,
> And her womb always enlarged with me.
> Why did I come forth from the womb to see labor and sorrow,
> That my days should be consumed with shame?
>   (Jeremiah 20:14–18)

It's not easy to explain, but despite all my inner turmoil, I felt compelled to continue to share the gospel. I didn't hide my struggles, but I didn't want to hide what I was learning about Jesus, either.

There is almost nothing about how I started in the ministry that I would recommend to anyone else. I was completely new to the things of the Spirit, and I just didn't know a better way. I started to rent hotel rooms, lodges, and any other place available to rent. I preached in dark alleys and on street corners, and I knocked on doors, inviting people to church on Sundays. I handed out thousands of flyers each week to advertise my services. I was surprised and thrilled when any new person attended. With time there were at least thirty people who attended regularly. Every day I had prayed that the Lord would save me from my turmoil. Then, out of nowhere, Jesus finally reached His hand down to pull me up.

One day after a service, two friends needed a ride to a beauty supply store. I drove them there and waited in the car. After about fifteen minutes of sitting in the car, I got tired of waiting and went inside. This was probably the only time in my life that my impatience has worked for me instead of against me.

When I entered the store, I met a girl in a rose-colored smock who was standing at the door and greeting customers as they entered. She smiled and it was all over for me! I tried not to stare at her but could not help myself. She started to blush, and one of my friends noticed. From that moment on I had a sudden and irrepressible need for beauty supplies that I would never use!

For the next few weeks I stopped by the shop once a week, hoping to see her, although I had lost the self-confidence to ask out a girl as pretty as she was. A few weeks later, one of the friends I drove to the store (thank God for friends) invited the girl in the rose-colored smock to my house for my birthday party. Amazingly, she showed up, and the rest, as they say, is history.

God had used a girl to draw me into chapel services years earlier. And it would take the woman of my dreams to pull me out of the deepest depression of my life caused by my zeal and seeming inability to keep my mouth shut. I guess I didn't care enough about myself to fully snap out of it. But I thought if someone as beautiful as this girl sees something in me, there must be hope for me.

We were married nine months later.

I don't know what God is going to use as His hand to pull you up out of the water. All I know is that He who sits on high looks low. If you are willing to grab your help when it comes, His arm is never too short to save!

Summary

- Everything important in life depends on our reaching the other side of our fears.
- Spiritual muscle is often built under the weight of intense opposition.
- God may not come when you want Him, but He is always right on time!
- It's one thing to be aware of evils. It's another thing entirely to let them become your focus.
- If you can acknowledge God while you are still inside the storm, you are already on your way out.

Self-Analysis

1. Reflect on the idea that a teacher is quiet during a test, and consider how you have responded to God's silence in the past.
2. Have you ever felt like God sent you into a storm? What was the result?
3. Did you handle your last storm with rejoicing or complaining?

4. How have you allowed fear to keep you from an opportunity?
5. What action do you need to take today? Realize that it may be rejoicing in God's love and acceptance of you.

SIX

LEPERS WHO DID NOT STOP

Now it happened as He went to Jerusalem that He passed through the midst of Samaria and Galilee. Then as He entered a certain village, there met Him ten men who were lepers, who stood afar off. And they lifted up their voices and said, "Jesus, Master, have mercy on us!"

So when He saw them, He said to them, "Go, show yourselves to the priests." And so it was that as they went, they were cleansed.

And one of them, when he saw that he was healed, returned, and with a loud voice glorified God, and fell down on his face at His feet, giving Him thanks. And he was a Samaritan.

So Jesus answered and said, "Were there not ten cleansed? But where are the nine? Were there not any found who returned to give glory to God except this foreigner?" And He said to him, "Arise, go your way. Your faith has made you well."

(LUKE 17:11–19)

Polling graduating high school classes for annual yearbook awards is gradually fading. The traditional categories range from serious to funny: most likely to succeed, most likely to be president, most likely to end up on a farm, most likely to be mistaken for a parent, and so forth.

In Luke 17 we will focus on a man who would certainly not have won a coveted most-likely award. Out of his nine Jewish companions, this foreigner would have been voted the least likely to embrace a Jewish Messiah and the least likely to bloom above his friends, but this is exactly what he did.

God has a penchant for using people whom most would reject and rejecting people whom most would not expect. Here are just a few unlikely people in Scripture: Noah, who developed a drinking problem; Abraham, who was too old; Jacob, a liar; Leah, who was ugly; Gideon, who was afraid; Samson, a womanizer; Moses, a murderer; Rahab, a prostitute; David, an adulterer; Jonah, who ran from God; Elijah, a depressive; John the Baptist, who ate bugs; Matthew, a tax collector; Peter, who denied Christ; and Paul, a killer of Christians.

We are going to take a trip with ten lepers to discover the journey is as important as the destination. All ten received a miraculous healing, but it would be the least likely man who hit the spiritual jackpot.

Now it happened as He went to Jerusalem that He passed through the midst of Samaria and Galilee.

This occurred on Jesus' final journey to Jerusalem. He would soon sweat droplets of blood at the foot of the Mount of Olives in a garden called Gethsemane. Afterward He hung naked on the cross and experienced ultimate abandonment to redeem humanity. But before He arrived in Jerusalem, He chose to travel through Samaria and Galilee.

There was a long, bitter history between Jews and Samaritans. The animosity was so great that most Pharisees would not even walk through Samaria. They stretched their journeys by miles, crossing the Jordan and going through Perea in order to bypass Samaria all together. Unlike His Jewish counterparts, Jesus chose to travel along the border of the two regions, ignoring the likelihood He would encounter this hostile ethnic group.

Then as He entered a certain village, there met Him ten men who were lepers

Evangelist Beth Moore tells a story of her attempt to visit a leper colony in India. From her early days of studying the Bible, she had a desire to minister to lepers. Finally, her golden opportunity arrived.

As soon as she entered the area, she knew a leper colony was near because an unpleasant odor permeated the air. It could be smelled several blocks away, where her hotel was situated. Undeterred by the scent and fueled by her passion to minister to the neediest, she arrived at the entrance to the colony.

When she made it to the gate, she had every intention of going in. She attempted to enter three times but was overcome each time by the remarkably pungent odor that assaulted her. This stench was overpowering. As she stood outside the gate, she wondered how she could ever be effective in sharing the love of Jesus while throwing up at the same time. As much as she desired to enter the colony, her good intentions were overridden by her weak stomach. She did not go in.[1]

To understand this Bible narrative, we must understand that these ten lepers assaulted the senses of Jesus and His disciples in every possible way!

Who stood afar off.

Leprosy was a very contagious disease for which there was no known cure. Advanced leprosy often created oozing sores and tumor-like growths that emanated a foul, putrid smell. It disfigured bones, twisted limbs, curled fingers, and created a loss of sensation at nerve endings, which often led to the eventual loss of fingers and toes. Sometimes whole limbs went missing.

They had no antibiotics or medicines to treat the disease. So lepers were required by the Mosaic law to stay one hundred paces away from healthy people. They had to cry, "Unclean! Unclean!" with a loud voice to warn anyone who might stumble into their presence. The law commanded this to protect others from contamination and to save the larger community from the possibility of an epidemic.

On top of the medical concerns, all lepers were considered ceremonially unclean, which meant they were not allowed into the worship assembly. They were ostracized by society and often abandoned by their loved ones. It was not unusual for them to band together in groups to create their own isolated but tortured communities.

And they lifted up their voices

The phrasing "they lifted up their voices" is a gentle way of saying they shouted. They did not do this out of disrespect but because of the distance they had to maintain from others. Jesus had already healed one leper and everyone wanted to be the next, but this began to draw a lot of attention for reasons He did not approve (Matthew 8:1–3).

It seems people began to show up more to receive His miracles than they did to hear His message. After healing the leper as recorded in Matthew 8, He asked him not to tell anyone. But people tend to keep secrets to protect themselves, not others (Matthew 8:1–4). The leper didn't keep the secret, and news of Jesus' healing power spread like wildfire (Luke 5:15). We can't blame these lepers for wanting to meet Jesus and be healed too. They probably prayed daily for such an opportunity. And when the opportunity came, as it did in this passage, they were ready to seize it.

And said, "Jesus, Master, have mercy on us!"

As soon as they saw Jesus, they addressed Him as Master. The word translated "Master" is very rare in the New Testament. It is used to designate a commander or owner.[2] The word emphasizes total authority. By using this language, all ten men were submitting to Jesus as their ultimate authority, which resulted in one of the few explicitly stated mass healings in Scripture.

Instead of asking for money, like most lepers on the side of the road, these ten asked for mercy, which was what they most needed. We may be able to buy a bed but not sleep, a house but not a home, sex but not love, entertainment but not happiness, and medicine but not health. A person is not truly blessed, however, until he has something money can't buy. By this standard, Jesus was the wealthiest man who had ever lived. Amazingly, the more He shared, the wealthier He became.

So when He saw them, He said to them, "Go, show yourselves to the priests."

The ten men boldly addressed Jesus as their Master. If we are truly gold, we should not be put off if God requires an acid test. Jesus was not a pushover then, and He is not today. He offered them an opportunity to prove the authenticity of this confession.

If He were truly their Master, they would obey Him, although He would perform this miracle a lot differently than the one they had heard about. In the earlier miracle, He "put out His Hand and touched him" and said "be cleansed" (Luke 5:13). This time, however, there was no gentle touch. Their miracle was designed to happen only if they followed what He said. It is not that our obedience can ever make God love us more. Our obedience, however, is an indicator of how much we truly love Him (John 14:15).

Here is where the request got thorny. Why were these ten lepers told to show themselves to the priests? Jesus had not yet healed them. Normally, a person would approach the priests after he was healed, not before.

It was the priests who had declared these men unclean and banned them. The last thing they wanted to do was see another priest. But true gospel submission doesn't come into play until there is some level of reluctance. No one would need to submit to another if they were always in perfect agreement. According to an old African proverb, but for the beauty of the rose, we also water the thorns. Submission always begins at the point of disagreement.

Remember, faith is spelled t-r-u-s-t. Faith is simply a heartfelt confidence so strong that we act on what God says even before we see the evidence of its wisdom. Faith is trusting with all our hearts before we see it in our hands. And these men had real faith and put it into action.

And so it was that as they went, they were cleansed.

Notice, their healing did not manifest the moment Jesus spoke to them or when they reached the priests. Some miracles happen along the journey. This is important to understand. I cannot predict if the trip to experiencing your miracle will be a short walk or a long one. All I know is that if you start moving in the direction God tells you to go, God's power will eventually show up and something big will happen.

And one of them, when he saw that he was healed, returned

The lepers looked at their hands and saw the sores were gone. They looked at their feet and saw the swelling and oozing had ceased. They felt their faces and found their skin was smooth. One man, however, had to stop. How could he continue to walk in the opposite direction, away from the person to whom he owed all this? I find it is not happy people who are thankful but rather thankful people who are happy.

Perhaps the nine Jewish lepers did not return because they felt entitled to their healing due to their heritage and nationality, but not this man. He knew his new life was completely dependent upon and wrapped up in God's mercy. He could not in good conscience keep walking without first going back to give thanks.

Some people need to stop reading right here and take a moment to lift their hands toward heaven and say, "Thank You for waking me up this morning. Thank You for the air I breathe, the sensations I feel, the food I taste, the rain I smell, and the sounds I hear. Thank You that I am still in my right mind. I may not have everything I want, but I have more than I deserve. I say thank You!"

And with a loud voice glorified God

This man had spent his life shouting "Unclean! Unclean!" one hundred paces away from everyone he came across. He spoke loudly because this is what was required of him. Some people come off as a little more aggressive, not because they are bad but because of the distance between themselves, their dreams, and all they had to fight through in their lives to get where they are. After this leper received his healing, he continued to speak loudly. But for the first time, his raspy, boisterous voice spoke words of praise and adoration instead of warning.

How is it that we spend so much of our lives being loud about everything unclean, but after God touches us, we talk about it in whispers? How is that we can be so on fire for the Devil, with uncleanliness oozing out of our lives, mouths, feet, and hands, yet after God cleanses us, we are suddenly too sophisticated to live for God with a shout?

Use your imagination and really think about this. What would your life be like tomorrow morning if you woke up with only the things you thanked God for today? Would most of the people you loved be gone? Would parts of your body that you tell yourself you hate so much suddenly be gone? Would half your stuff and job be gone? I would rather thank God a day too soon than an hour too late.

And fell down on his face at His feet, giving Him thanks.

Falling to the ground was the highest way to give honor and respect in the ancient world. This lone leper fell on his freshly cleansed face to glorify God. This man would not receive a blessing from God that he was unwilling to give back.

God gives all of us twenty-four hours every day, but many of us spend half of it complaining about the time we don't have and the things we can't do. Try to go a whole twenty-four hours without complaining. Most of us would be surprised by how negative we and the people around us are. Then watch how your life begins to change.

And he was a Samaritan.

This man had the highest hurdles to overcome. He was a Samaritan. He belonged to a people with an ancient hatred for the Jews, which happened to be Jesus' lineage. Attitudes between Jews and Samaritans were as strong as the worst political and racial divides in parts of our country today.

All ten men were separated from the population because of their leprosy. But only this man would be required to remain separated from those in this neighborhood after his healing because of his nationality. Amazingly, the person with the greatest ethnic and religious justifications to stay away from Jesus was the only one to return and give Him glory.

Never allow your past or anything in your background to keep you from Jesus. People may hold it against you, but not the carpenter from Galilee.

So Jesus answered and said, "Were there not ten cleansed? But where are the nine?"

Jesus was stating the obvious. Just a short while ago, all ten lepers were diseased and unclean. When they followed His instructions, they were healed. But only one felt compelled to return to thank Him. I wonder if the nine were thinking, *Yes, Jesus, You healed me, and I appreciate what You did, but I heard You laid hands on others and You didn't even touch me.* Or perhaps they thought, *Yes, Jesus, I appreciate Your healing me, but why did I have to walk first? Others got it on the spot.* Few things destroy our experience with God more than comparing ourselves with others and looking for flaws. The nine lepers remind me of a story about a large dog.

The dog walked into a butcher shop carrying a wallet in his mouth. He put it down in front of the meat case.

The butcher jokingly asked, "What is it, boy? Want to buy some meat? What kind of meat? Liver? Bacon? Steak?"

The dog woofed at the word *steak*.

"How much? A half-pound? One pound?"

The dog woofed at one pound.

The butcher wrapped up a pound of steak and took the money out of the wallet. Amazed at this transaction, he decided to follow the dog to see what he was going to do next.

The dog entered an apartment building blocks away, walked up three flights of stairs, and scratched at a door.

The door swung open and an angry man shouted at the dog.

The butcher yelled, "Stop! This is the most intelligent animal I have ever seen!"

"Intelligent?" says the man. "This is the third time this week he's forgotten his key!"

Some people will always find a reason to be critical and ungrateful, no matter how great the deed! Let's not be like the man in this story or the nine lepers who did not return. Instead, be grateful for everything we receive.

A writer once said, "Ingratitude is a crime more despicable than revenge: revenge is returning evil for evil, but ingratitude returns evil for good."[3] Gratitude begins where a sense of entitlement ends.[4]

"Were there not any found who returned to give glory to God except this foreigner?"

Jesus questioned why the non-Jewish man was the only one to return and give thanks. I heard Desmond Tutu say once in a speech, "All those pictures of the shepherd carrying this baby sheep in his arms are absolutely false. I grew up in an agricultural society and the baby sheep never run away. They are too hungry for the mother's milk. It's the old sheep. It's the matted sheep. It's those who have been around for a long time. Those are the ones who start to wander."

And He said to him, "Arise, go your way. Your faith has made you well."

The eighteenth-century French writer Voltaire declared, "The best is the enemy of the good."[5] Ten lepers received an outward physical healing. This was good. But the best was hiding behind a door named thankfulness, and only one found it. There is a level of peace and blessing only the grateful will receive, and all without it will never understand.

This Samaritan didn't settle for a healing. He went for the blessing. The Greek word used for *well* in this verse is different from the word used earlier for *healed*. Jesus healed and repaired the skin of all the lepers, but only one leper was made well. The grateful man not only changed on the outside, but his transformation occurred also on the inside. Emotional health does not mean we deny that pain exists. It just means that it no longer controls our lives.

A broken heart is far more complicated to heal than a broken bone. It also takes a lot more time. The Bible says, "The spirit of a man will sustain him in sickness, but who can bear a broken spirit?" (Proverbs 18:14). God is telling us that if our hearts are made healthy and strong, we can endure anything. If our hearts grow critical and bitter they become weak and even the smallest things become hard to bear. Life will become a lot clearer when we pay as much attention to the beauty inside our hearts as on our faces.

My Story

My heart was on the mend. I began to square my shoulders, there was an easy gait in my step, there was light in my eyes, and the wind was at my back once again. I leased a storefront space about one hundred feet from a crack corner in Washington, DC, to house our new church. A homeless shelter was diagonally across the street from our building. Unemployed men leaned on buildings and drank from brown bags most of the day, and prostitutes worked the area. This was the place I always dreamed of serving and the type of place I felt a church could have the greatest impact.

But there was a great deal of construction work that needed to be done before we could move in and hold worship services there. At the end of each day of painting, putting up drywall, and getting the building ready, my clothes were soaked through with blood. Even the edges of my white tube socks turned faded pink from the mixture of blood and sweat from working in the summer heat.

I had been spotting in my clothes, at the base of my spine, off and on for a few years. It was growing progressively worse and more painful. A doctor explained it was an infected varicose vein and could be managed.

I was in good health generally. I worked out regularly, but I think the years of inner turmoil eventually affected me physically. My mind and body were more connected than I wanted to believe. I sought a second opinion and was finally told I had developed a pilonidal cyst.

I had no health insurance at the time, and the cyst grew to several inches deep and roughly seven inches long. By the time I could afford to see a surgeon, he described it as the biggest cyst he had ever seen in that part of a person's body. After several surgeries, doctors told me there was nothing more they could do. They advised me to keep the area clean and to learn to live with it.

This condition required me to take at least three baths a day, and sometimes more during the summer months, to prevent infection. After my baths, my wife would pack the wound with gauze and hydrogen peroxide. I walked around with a pillow, so that when I sat, less pressure was put on the area, though the pain was still constant.

My illness was difficult, but I was so focused on the opportunity of serving my church, I learned to live with the pain. My wife went back to college and started working in a department store. I received a small salary from the church. I had made some good financial investments over the years, and they covered the rest of our expenses. We were excited and ready to change the world!

The church had a core group of about ten people with good jobs. They helped to support the church and the work we were doing. I never really thought about how I would fund things before opening the church. I thought a call from God was all I needed. We filled the seventy-seat building whenever the shelter leader brought the long-term stays with him, but normally we had only about thirty attendees. I was both grateful and amazed that any-one showed up to listen.

Soon I began cashing out my investments to make ends meet, and my pilonidal cyst grew worse. Slowly, some of our core members moved on. The rest of the congregation was comprised of people on fixed incomes who were recovering from drugs and long-term alcohol abuse. It was not long before I had to close the doors of the church.

I'll never forget my final day when I took a final look around and returned the keys to our storefront. My mouth was so dry, I could feel myself swallow. My head felt light. I had a picture of Martin Luther King behind my desk. I stared at him for about forty-five minutes, and I began to think that maybe I had gotten this whole God thing wrong. *Perhaps God can't be known the way I think I know Him. Maybe the universe is more like the proverbial clock created by the divine clockmaker. Perhaps God sends us occasional rays of light, but the rest is up to us.*

As far as I was concerned, I had failed in ministry for the second time. I was a little more than thirty years old, and my oldest son had just been born. I was getting too old and too much was at risk for me not to have my feet firmly planted on the ground so I could take care of my family.

Every time the surgeons operated to remove the cyst, it would grow back. I interviewed for several full-time positions to no avail. The need to go home to bathe several times a day, coupled with an inability to sit for more than thirty minutes at a time, was a deal breaker for most employers. I continued to write and perform odd jobs.

After closing the church, a few of the remaining core members convinced me to at least hold a Bible study at a friend's apartment in Virginia. I planned to continue this Bible study until everyone transitioned and found a new church.

I studied more intensely than ever. I read everyone from Augustine to Karl Barth to Martin Luther. I continued with John Bunyan, Charles Hodge, C. S. Lewis, Francis Schaeffer, and others. My hope was that one of these men would straighten me out and cure me of this all-consuming, ridiculous desire to truly know God.

I was doing a little investing and freelance writing to help make ends meet. The days were tough, but I began having difficulty sleeping at night. I had to sleep on my stomach, not to aggravate the cyst, but I had gotten accustomed to that. This insomnia had nothing to do with my body but rather a relentless gnawing in my soul.

I already had two strikes, and I could not afford one more. I was not a kid anymore. I would ask myself, *What possesses me to think I could ever do anything meaningful for God, much less be a minister? In this modern age, is it even possible to build a church based on the authority of God's Word alone?*

One evening I was walking around a mall and saw a Michael Jordan poster in a store window. I purchased it and brought it home and hung it in my garage. It had his picture and a quote: "I've missed more than 9000 shots in my career. I've lost almost 300 games. 26 times, I've been trusted to take the game winning shot and missed. I've failed over and over and over again in my life. And that is why I succeed." This resonated with me.

I decided I needed to find a way to either silence or follow the voice within. I don't recommend this, but I decided to go so far out that only God could save me if I was wrong. I took cash advances on my credit cards and rented a high school auditorium in Virginia, about fifteen minutes from my home. The plan was to try one more time and see what God would do. Twelve people attended the first service. They were mostly people from my Bible study.

Within a few weeks, attendance increased to around thirty. To my amazement, in only a few months, one hundred people were attending regularly. I began to think maybe I was not crazy after all! My highest imaginable goal in ministry was to one day have a five-hundred-member church. We eventually grew to more than two hundred members. I was nearly halfway there. Words cannot explain the relief and satisfaction I felt.

I continued to seek treatment for the cyst. I stood as I preached, kneeled as I read, and used several pillows when I had to sit. Everything may not have gone exactly as I would have planned, but despite the cyst, I was appreciative of all God had done. I had seen several surgeons and had many surgeries to cut out the cyst, burn it, staple the wound around it, and even recut the skin. But all these efforts failed, and the cyst remained infected.

I couldn't do all the things I wanted to do with my wife and kids. I also wanted to get a job apart from the ministry, until the church grew stronger. Some in the church criticized me for not doing more. I began to feel boxed in and decided it was time to fast and pray. I needed to find out why this illness was so persistent.

As I sought answers concerning my health, God reminded me of the events at Howard University, which had a deeper impact than I had realized. I began to confess to God my bottled-up feelings of rejection, grief, and self-loathing. Then I realized something I had never thought before. Maybe my problems were not only physical but spiritual. I had also read many Kenneth Hagin books while in college and took his advice to use Jesus' name to take authority over the spiritual forces that my pent-up emotions may have released. As soon as I did, all I can say is it felt as if something shifted.

I was scheduled for another surgery, but deep down inside I knew something had changed. I believed things would be different in this next visit to the doctor. In the presurgical appointment, the surgeon inspected the incision. For the first time in years, it was not swollen, bleeding, or red. It was totally closed. The surgery was canceled!

This healing became a light at the end of our tunnel. It gave my wife and me a renewed confidence that God was with us. I decided to go back to school. I was only four courses away from my undergraduate degree, but I didn't want to go back to Howard to finish.

I felt a nudge inside my heart not to attend a new school to complete my business degree. I did something I never imagined possible. I applied to a graduate program at a highly regarded Christian university. They accepted me without my having to complete my final undergraduate classes.

All along, God knew what He had ahead for me was better than what had passed. I then went on to earn a doctorate. I can't think about this without being reminded of the words of one of the prophets, "I will repay you for the years the locusts have eaten—the great locust and the young locust, the other locusts and the locust swarm—my great army that I sent among you" (Joel 2:25 NIV).

This period coincided with the peak of the housing market in the mid-2000s, before the market crash. My wife and I decided to sell our townhome. Not only did we recover from years of financial struggle, but we invested the windfall and were well on our way to financial independence. I was not only physically healed, I was being made whole.

My wife and I finally had the resources to make our first trip back to her birthplace, Ethiopia. My kids were able to meet their uncle and extended family for the first time. While there, we had a marriage ceremony in keeping with her traditions and culture.

We had come full circle. It appeared the worst was behind us as a family. But unbeknownst to me, although we might have passed some tests, a final exam was on the way.

Mother Teresa observed, "The biggest disease today is not leprosy or tuberculosis, but rather the feeling of being unwanted."[6] Facing rejection from others is painful but bearable. It's self-rejection that causes the greatest harm. My social leprosy came from my conviction that the God of the Bible was real even in a so-called post-Christian era. My "running sore" was the idea that Jesus was more than the founder of a religion but through Him God could be known, experienced, and understood.

Jesus had not only healed me but was intent on making me whole. He was building the inner confidence I needed to help me stop being afraid of being so different. As I grow older my greatest fear is no longer being different but becoming ordinary, like everyone else. Like the lepers, I cried to the Lord and "in the day when I cried out, [He] answered me, and made me bold with strength in my soul" (Psalm 138:3).

There are a lot of people who made better choices than I have, are smarter than I am, more gifted than I am, with greater understanding than I have, but you will not find many people more grateful than I am. The German theologian Meister Eckhart said, "If the only prayer you ever say in your entire life is thank you, it will be enough."[7]

Summary

- Obedience does not make God love us more, but it's a great indicator of how much we love God.
- Healing did not manifest the moment Jesus spoke; it occurred only after obeying His instruction.
- Some people spend their lives being loud about things that are unclean, but after God rebuilds their lives, they barely whisper about it.
- Imagine what your life would be like tomorrow if you only woke up with the things you thanked God out loud for today.
- When you recognize the power of God in your life, you can't help but fall on your face at the Master's feet and give thanks.

Self-Analysis

1. Could it be your unwillingness to thank God has impacted the extent of healing in your life?
2. How often during a day do you consciously thank God for something?
3. What are three things you believe you deserve but have yet to receive?
4. Are you relatively healthy physically but emotionally angry about a few things? If so, what are you angry about?
5. What do you believe God wants you to do with your anger today?

SEVEN

THE PEOPLE GOD HAD TO STOP

But Jesus went to the Mount of Olives.

Now early in the morning He came again into the temple, and all the people came to Him; and He sat down and taught them. Then the scribes and Pharisees brought to Him a woman caught in adultery. And when they had set her in the midst, they said to Him, "Teacher, this woman was caught in adultery, in the very act. Now Moses, in the law, commanded us that such should be stoned. But what do You say?" This they said, testing Him, that they might have something of which to accuse Him. But Jesus stooped down and wrote on the ground with His finger, as though He did not hear.

So when they continued asking Him, He raised Himself up and said to them, "He who is without sin among you, let him throw a stone at her first." And again He stooped down and wrote on the ground. Then those who heard it, being convicted by their conscience, went out one by one, beginning with the oldest even to the last. And Jesus was left alone, and the woman standing in the midst. When Jesus had raised Himself up and saw no one but the woman, He said to her, "Woman, where are those accusers of yours? Has no one condemned you?"

She said, "No one, Lord."

And Jesus said to her, "Neither do I condemn you; go and sin no more."

(JOHN 8:1–11)

I n *Narrative of the Life of Frederick Douglass, an American Slave,* Frederick Douglass described slavery firsthand. He was born a slave in Talbot County, Maryland, in 1818. When he was around twenty years old, he escaped slavery and became the great abolitionist and social reformer we all love.

His 1845 autobiographical book is arguably the most famous of all the narratives written by any former slave. He described the facts of his life not only with eloquence but with extraordinary clarity. American slavery was an institution established expressly for the profit of the ruling class; its undertones brought out the worst in people and manifested as brutal restrictions, racial privilege, and unchecked sexual exploitation.

"Unmanageable" slaves were often whipped and sold off as a warning to other slaves. "Children from seven to ten years old, of both sexes, almost naked, might be seen all seasons of the year."[1] Often the most heartless men were selected to be overseers. Slaves worked long hours with little sleep. They had no beds and only a few had worn, inadequate blankets. Slaves were often treated like farm animals.

Laws at that time guaranteed that mixed-race children, such as Douglass, were to be treated as slaves, like their mothers. Over time Douglass was selected to work in the house of his master, who actually may have been his father. But he was not able to confirm this. His mother was sold off, and he remembered meeting her only a few times. Their meetings were uncomfortable because she was only able to see him at night. When she died, he commented he "never . . .

enjoyed, to any considerable extent, her soothing presence, her tender and watchful care." To him, her death was like the "death of a stranger." Contrary to popular stereotypes and oversimplifications of the definitions of blackness, Douglass believed mixed-race slaves were much worse off than other enslaved counterparts, primarily due to living under the bitter and watchful eye of the wife of the master who may have illegitimately fathered them.

A master often sold off his mixed-race children "out of deference to the feelings of his white wife." Her husband's slave children were constant reminders of his adultery and fueled all types of feelings of inadequacy and insecurity. If the mixed-race children were not sold off, Douglass believed they suffered the worst of all the slaves on the plantation.

The eighth chapter of the gospel of John paints a picture of a fierce standoff between Jesus and the religious rulers and involved a woman who had been caught in an act of adultery. Many scholars believe the woman here was a prostitute or a sex slave. While the religious authorities intended to place her on trial, Jesus turned this outdoor courtroom upside down.

It is not unusual to find someone who will fight for his own rights, but it is rare to find a person who would do as Jesus did and stand up for another's rights at his own risk. Instead of only this woman being placed on trial, Jesus put on trial everyone who was inclined to pick up a stone, along with her. In the following narrative, Jesus stopped to protect a woman from the crowd and the crowd from itself.

But Jesus went to the Mount of Olives.

The Mount of Olives was a two-and-a-half-mile-long mountain ridge that extended across the eastern side of Jerusalem.[2] It was heavily wooded with olive trees, and at its foot was the Garden of Gethsemane, Jesus' favorite place to pray. Critical moments of Jesus' life occurred here. Most famously it was in this garden that Jesus fought severe depression, deep betrayal, and the horror of the crucifixion. His last visit ended with His sweating drops of blood and with His arrest (Mark 14:32–50).

Jesus had a lifestyle of intense daily prayer (Hebrews 5:7). He would often get up before it was fully light and go off into nature to be alone with His Father (Mark 1:35). Although the disciples never asked Him to show them how to teach and preach, His prayer life was so admirable that they asked Him to teach them how to pray (Luke 11:1–4). Martin Luther often struggled with depression and understood the need of time alone with God. To that end, he said, "To be a Christian without prayer is no more possible than to be alive without breathing."[3]

People often say they can't find enough time to pray. I have found I don't have enough time *not* to pray. I can pray either before my day to help me stay on course, or I can pray at night, asking God to fix the regrets of the day. Either way, prayer will occupy my time.

Now early in the morning He came again into the temple

Jesus spent a lot of time teaching and worshipping God with other believers in the temple (Matthew 26:55). From the time He was a boy, whenever He was in Jerusalem He was in the temple as long as the doors were open (Luke 2:46). Today, many people find it burdensome to attend church, but this was not at all Jesus' mind-set. In the corporate worship environment, we have an opportunity to demonstrate our love not only for our Father but for one another.

It's one of my life's greatest privileges to be part of a weekly gathering that, as a whole, is greater than the sum of all its individual parts. Helen Keller observed, "Alone we can do so little. Together we can do so much."[4] As we deepen our relationship with God, we learn conversely to deepen our relationships with His sacred community. If we refuse to love our brothers and sisters, whom we can see, how can we say we truly love God, whom we cannot see (1 John 4:20)? The church is not a place for perfect people but a shelter for the recovering and hurting.

And all the people came to Him; and He sat down and taught them.

Jesus taught more than He did anything else, including the working of miracles. He was often referred to as teacher rather than a preacher or miracle worker (John 13:13). Teaching and preaching are both necessary but not the same. T. F. Hodge explained the difference: "The difference between preaching and teaching is one makes you feel good and the other makes you grow."[5]

A quick scan of the Gospels reveals that Jesus tended to sit more than He stood while speaking. If He preached while standing and taught while sitting, we could conclude that inspirational preaching was very important, but teaching was a greater priority to Him. This is in line with what the Bible says about teaching: "Wisdom is the principal thing; therefore get wisdom. And in all your getting, get understanding" (Proverbs 4:7).

Many came to Jesus out of deep personal needs, some out of curiosity, and others from a desire to learn and grow. Whatever their reasons, people flocked to Him, and no one left the encounter unimpacted (Matthew 10:34–35). Someone said, "Light yourself on fire with passion for God and people will come from miles to watch you burn."[6] But everyone did not embrace this new fire, and they were about to put it to the test.

Then the scribes and Pharisees brought to Him a woman caught in adultery.

The scribes were teachers who spent their lives studying, transcribing, and writing commentaries on the law of Moses. In the time of Jesus, most of scribes had pharisaical leanings. The Pharisees were a popular religious movement that had become the most influential religious party in the early first century. The scribes and Pharisees often presented the law in a way that captured the letter but missed the spirit.[7]

And when they had set her in the midst

The adulterous woman was probably half-dressed, bruised from rough handling, and dragged kicking and screaming to Jesus. While adultery is painfully wrong, at least it appears in this passage as if she tried to do it privately. Today, however, we print T-shirts, write books, air commercials, and post all kinds of social media to galvanize people behind our sins and publicly shame anyone who calls us out. The only thing people seem to be ashamed of today is righteousness.

They said to Him, "Teacher, this woman was caught in adultery, in the very act."

"In the very act"? Those who know a little something about the birds and bees might wonder how it's possible to catch a woman in the act of adultery and not catch the man. Something does not add up. How is it the man was absent from this hearing?

Some commentators suggested the reason they did not bring the man was because he was one of them, either a scribe or a Pharisee. If the religious leaders were the adulterous woman's customers, this would be consistent with human nature. If one of us does it, we call it a mistake, but if one of them does it, they should be whipped and hanged, or in this case stoned. Jesus saw through the masquerade and would have no part in it.

"Now Moses, in the law, commanded us that such should be stoned. But what do You say?"

Facing insincere questioners is mentally exhausting. It is easier to face a group's honest hatred than try to address its artificiality. These leaders cared nothing for the adulterous woman. She was just a prop to ensnare Jesus. Their only goal was to win and to do so at any cost. It was very much like today's political climate. No one cares who they harm as long as their side wins.

The Pharisees and scribes began by flattering Jesus, calling Him "teacher." On the surface flattery looks like respect, but only in the way a wolf looks like a dog. This confrontation with Jesus was a well-thought-out plan. If Jesus had been an ordinary man, He would certainly have fallen prey to it. But as events turned out, this would not be the last time the religious leaders underestimated Him.

Unlike the scholars who posed the question, Jesus not only knew God's Word, He was the manifestation and fulfillment of every word God had ever spoken (Matthew 5:17). The law of Moses specifically addressed adultery: "If a man is found lying with a woman married to a husband, then *both* of them shall die" (Deuteronomy 22:22). But notice that Moses said "both of them." To avoid any confusion, the lawgiver even reiterated this further in the same verse: "*the man that lay with the woman, and the woman*; so you shall put away the evil from Israel" (italics mine).

The law clearly stated both the man and the woman should die, but these Pharisees and scribes brought only the woman to Jesus. By bringing only her, the experts of the law violated the very law they presumed to uphold. They embraced only half the truth, the half that supported their point. As Benjamin Franklin pointed out, "Half the truth is often a great lie."[8]

This they said, testing Him, that they might have something of which to accuse Him.

The scenario was a catch-22. If Jesus approved the application of the Mosaic law that required they stone her, He would violate Roman law; namely, that under Roman law Jews did not have the right to put anyone to death. If Jesus did not approve the stoning of the adulterous woman, He would be in violation of the Mosaic law, and charges could be brought against Him before the Sanhedrin, the highest Jewish council during the time of the Roman occupation of Judea.

Clearly the religious establishment was looking for a way to invalidate Jesus' teaching, which was revolutionary and threatened their control over all religious matters affecting the Jews.[9] Later, this counsel chose to arrest, condemn, and refer Jesus to Pilate as the ultimate step in terminating His ministry.

But Jesus stooped down and wrote on the ground with His finger, as though He did not hear.

As far as the religious leaders were concerned, they had Jesus in a lose-lose scenario. There was little wiggle room, and they were ready to pounce on whatever He said and whichever course He chose. But Jesus was unfazed. He refused to give them the gratification of an immediate response. He looked away and ignored them. A meaningful silence is often more powerful than words. Jesus has not changed. I am so thankful for the many times He has ignored my ill-advised questions.

I imagine Jesus thinking, *You guys want to play in people's dirt, then let's get dirty.* He bent down and wrote on the ground with His finger, just as His finger was used to write the original Ten Commandments in stone (Exodus 31:18). By the Maccabean period of the second century BC, single letters of the Hebrew alphabet were used to represent each of the Ten Commandments. I picture Jesus writing an *aleph*, then a *beth*, a *gimel*, a *daleth*, and a *he*. These five letters represented the first five commandments. It would not take very long for Him to draw these letters in the dirt. Maybe just a little longer than it would take us to write the first five letters of our alphabet. When they continued to press Him, He paused and responded.

So when they continued asking Him, He raised Himself up and said to them, "He who is without sin among you, let him throw a stone at her first."

The religious leaders assumed Jesus' silence meant He was stumped. They failed to realize they were fighting way outside their weight class.

Timing is everything. They were trying to trap Jesus, but He flipped the script and was about to trap them.

In effect He said, "Okay, you can stone her, but here is the caveat. Look in the mirror first." Jesus wasn't denying the woman's sin. He simply shifted the focus from her sins to the sins of those in the crowd who were so intent on stoning her. When dealing with sin, it is always better to use a mirror instead of a microscope.

The problem was they wanted to prosecute a woman for her sin without considering their own. When Jesus did not follow suit, it was not that He was rejecting God's moral standards, but rather He was jealously guarding them from abuse. Jesus was nobody's fool!

And again He stooped down and wrote on the ground.

When Jesus bent down this second time, I imagine His writing the commandments on the second tablet of the Ten Commandments: *waw*, *zayin*, *heth*, *teth*, and *yod*. By the time He got to the last commandment, which focuses on the sins of desire, people started clearing their voices. The letter *yod* represented "You shall not covet your neighbor's wife." Uh-oh!

Perhaps those willing to pick up stones had sins that were less obvious to others, but the law was much like a pane of glass. If you broke the smallest part of it, you broke the whole thing (James 2:10). They lived lives of outward obedience to the Mosaic law but completely missed the requirements it laid on the heart (Matthew 15:19; Romans 7:17). These Pharisees and scribes may not have done exactly what this woman did, but if they only desired to, they were just as guilty before God.

Like the woman caught in adultery, we have all done things,

said things, and gone places we should not have. What's amazing about Jesus is that although He was the only one with the moral authority to condemn her, He refused to do so. As the Bible says, "God did not send His Son into the world to condemn the world, but that the world through Him might be saved" (John 3:17).

Then those who heard it, being convicted by their conscience

Conscience is like a lion that can't bite, but it never stops roaring. But the moment we stop responding to our consciences, we lose the essence of what separates us from the rest of the animal kingdom. The crowd in the temple that day may have misunderstood the law, but when Jesus pressured them they were at least honest with themselves. It may be wise not to be overly transparent with everyone at times, but we should never lie to ourselves.

Went out one by one, beginning with the oldest even to the last

Age and experience have a way of tempering our self-righteousness. If you live long enough, you will discover you are not much better than those whom you find guilty of the "worst" sins (Matthew 15:19). We have all sinned and are all in need of the Savior. This does not mean we don't call things what they are, but we must all remember, "There go I but for the grace of God."[10]

And Jesus was left alone, and the woman standing in the midst.

When we are alone with Jesus, we are never alone. All the woman's accusers had backed away into the distance, and what follows is one of the greatest pictures of peace in the Bible. All the voices of condemnation had been silenced and sent away. The only voice left to be heard in her life belonged to Jesus, and whom the Son chose to set free that day would be free indeed (John 8:36)!

This is the gospel story: Jesus bent down into the dirt to lift the woman out of it. He does not treat us based on what we have been but on what He can make of us! Will you allow Him to do the same for you?

When Jesus had raised Himself up and saw no one but the woman, He said to her, "Woman, where are those accusers of yours? Has no one condemned you?"

This is the final time Jesus stood up, and He stood not as her condemner but as her redeemer. Somehow He sees our value despite our shame. Through His questioning He explained to the woman that she was no more sinful in the eyes of the law than those who at one point wanted to stone her. We must guard against judging others more harshly, just because their sins are different from our own.

She said, "No one, Lord." And Jesus said to her,
"Neither do I condemn you; go and sin no more."

Instead of discarding her, Jesus gave the woman the power to walk away from her life of sin. God does not redefine sin just because He loves us. Instead, He breaks its power in order to help us live more and more free of it. Satan knows your name but calls you by your sin. God knows your sin but calls you by your name.[11]

It would make no sense for Jesus to go through all the trouble of coming to Earth just to put us down. We were already down without Him. He came to Earth to pick us up and let us go. The following story captures the loving care that God wants to provide each of us.

Mark Reed of Camarillo, California, saw a sparrow hop through the open door and peck at the crumbs near his table. When the crumbs were gone, the sparrow hopped to the window ledge, spread its wings, and took flight. The bird's visit was brief. But then the sparrow crashed against a window pane and fell to the floor. The bird quickly recovered and tried again and crashed again. Mark got up and attempted to show the sparrow out the door, but the closer he got, the harder it threw itself against the pane. He nudged it with his hand. That sent the sparrow fluttering along the edge, hammering its beak against the glass. Finally, Mark reached out and caught the bird, folding his fingers around its wings and body. It weighed almost nothing. He thought of how powerless the vulnerable sparrow must have felt. At the door he released it and the sparrow sailed away. As Mark did with the sparrow, God takes us captive only to set us free.[12]

The most complex job God has in the universe is not protecting us from our enemies but protecting us from ourselves. Instead of destroying the woman caught in adultery, Jesus led her to freedom. The road God has each of us travel toward Him is not only about the destination but also the change the journey brings about. God has a special way of taking the broken pieces of our lives and turning them into His masterpieces.

My Story

After nine years of meeting twice a week in a high school auditorium, our congregation grew to a little more than two hundred people. We began to aggressively save to purchase a church building of our own. We decided to buy a warehouse unit about fifteen minutes from the high school.

The building was in a lower-income area, and many in my congregation had mixed emotions about moving there. But I was certain it was the right choice. The building was on a one-way street, concealed behind trees, with a storefront exterior. Its modest eighty-seven hundred square feet could seat roughly three hundred people in the main sanctuary and another hundred people on the second level. While the structure might not have been beautiful, it would be our own, and for that I was extremely excited.

When we completed the build-out, I felt after years of hard work, I was finally able to exhale. At our grand opening, the building was packed with people. But most who attended came out of curiosity. Little did I know many in the congregation had already decided to attend churches closer to their homes. Every week our attendance dwindled, until six months later, the congregation had shrunk from hundreds to fewer than thirty adults. For some it was the distance, for others it was the neighborhood, and some just wanted to follow the crowd.

The monthly mortgage payment of the new building was roughly $12,000. There was no way a congregation of thirty people could afford to pay this. My wife and I decided to put a lien on our home to buy us some time and keep the church afloat.

The church governing board was aware of the financial challenges, but I was unwilling to announce our financial needs to the few remaining congregants. Perhaps it was my pride, but I did not want not to put any financial pressure on the congregation. I felt if God had helped us move into the building, which I certainly knew He had, He would find a way for us to stay in it.

I was unsuccessful at the university. I had to shut down the Washington, DC, church. And this looked like the final pitch, a curve ball. And I was about to make a strike again. The only difference this time was I was older and knew whatever happened I would probably not recover. Either way, I concluded if somehow the God who raised Jesus from the dead and called me into the ministry was not real, it was best for me to face it now.

This was my moment of truth! If God had truly called me to this work, He would have to show Himself strong. Weeks passed, however, and things only got worse. I remained silent with the congregation about our circumstances and preached to an empty sanctuary and disheartened people every Sunday and Wednesday. I finally ran out of money to lend to the church, and I had to cut my losses for my family's sake. I asked our Realtor to put the brand-new church up for sale.

I was numb. I had run out of options and prayers. Solomon's words echoed in my mind: "Unless the LORD builds the house, they labor in vain who build it; unless the LORD guards the city, the watchman stays awake in vain. It is in vain for you to rise up early, to sit up late, to eat the bread of sorrows, for so He gives His beloved sleep" (Psalm 127:1–2). I resigned myself to the fact that the church would not survive unless God performed a miracle.

The Lord had been speaking to me through the Scriptures. In fact, the night before I asked the agent to put the building up for sale, God spoke to my heart only a part of Romans 4:19 from the NIV translation: "[Abraham] faced the fact his body was as good as dead." I felt the Lord was telling me to face the facts and deal with them squarely.

But the *Message* translation really brings the meaning of this verse to the surface:

> We call Abraham "father" not because he got God's attention by living like a saint, but because God made something out of Abraham when he was a nobody. Isn't that what we've always read in Scripture, God saying to Abraham, "I set you up as father of many peoples"? Abraham was first named "father" and then became a father because he dared to trust God to do what only God could do: raise the dead to life, with a word make some-thing out of nothing. When everything was hopeless, Abraham believed anyway, deciding to live not on the basis of what he saw he *couldn't* do but on what God said he *would* do. And so he was made father of a multitude of peoples. God himself said to him, "You're going to have a big family, Abraham!" (Romans 4:17–18)

"Raise the dead to life, with a word make something out of nothing" was exactly what God would have to do for our church to survive. The many failures in my ministry were not designed to harm me but to build me. As I said in chapter 5, we are never the same when we come out of a storm as when we went into the storm, and this is what the storm is really about.

God-reliance and self-reliance are utterly incompatible, and self-reliance had been my battle from day one. These early years of ministry reminded me of when I had a wart on my knuckle when I was a boy. The doctor started treatment by giving me an ointment, which did not work. Next he tried to burn it off. This also did not work. After the final burning treatment, the doctor pulled my father aside.

The appointment for the next visit came, and my father was quieter than usual on the ride to the doctor's office. When I entered the examination room, the doctor exchanged glances with my dad. My father grabbed my hand and the doctor produced a huge needle and stuck it straight into my knuckle. I screamed, "Daddy, how could you do this?" As the needle entered my knuckle, I felt my father had betrayed me, but he did what any loving father would do to ensure the well-being of his son. Just because it hurts does not mean the results won't be beautiful.

The needle only pierced the wart, but every part of my body protested. My father and the doctor never intended to harm me. They wanted the best for me and to rid me of what would only spread if left untreated.

Each failure since my final year in college was like a needle in my knuckle, medicine for my life. My failures helped strip me of my fierce independence and the stubborn notion that I could lead using my own resources. I am still a work in progress, but after several "needles to my knuckle," God's medicine had finally begun to take.

I completely humbled myself, let go, and admitted not only to God but more deeply than ever before to myself that, based on my own efforts I was like Abraham, as good as dead. As soon as I did this, it was as if God turned on a switch in my heart, and inexplicable confidence filled my heart. By the weekend, I told the agent I had changed my mind about listing our property. When Sunday rolled around, I preached with an assurance I could not explain. And the church responded like never before.

The number of attendees began to explode. Within weeks, we increased from thirty members to a hundred. Within a few months we were back to two hundred members. The rapid growth continued. In 2008 we had fewer than thirty members, but by 2011 we had a congregation of more than one thousand. I began to minister at four Sunday services to accommodate all the people who attended.

We leased a second building to serve our many children. We began a college to better serve our leaders. People had to be turned away because our facility could not hold everyone who came for our services.

By 2012 we purchased and renovated a warehouse directly across the street and turned it into a thousand-seat sanctuary. We thought that building would be large enough for us forever. By the first Sunday we had to hold two services and eventually three to meet the needs of the crowds.

In 2013 and 2014 we were celebrated as one of the fastest growing churches in the country.[13] That may not be a big deal for some, but to me it was as miraculous as God's parting the Red Sea for the children of Israel. The words of the apostle Paul are the only way I can explain anything God has done in my life, "My grace is sufficient for you, for My strength is made perfect in weakness" (2 Corinthians 12:9).

God's power works best not in people who think they are

strong but in people who understand their weakness and limitations. Some people ask me how I grew my church to become so large in our part of the country, but the honest answer is, I don't think I grew my church—it grew me.

Summary

- What's amazing about Jesus is that although He is perfect, He is compassionate enough not to reject us.
- Jesus wants to quiet every voice in our hearts that doesn't sound like His.
- Jesus doesn't treat us based on what we are but on what He has designed us to become!
- God takes us captive only to set us free.
- Inherent in every word from God is the power for its realization.

Self-Analysis

1. In what ways has prayer or the lack of it impacted a recent decision?
2. Can you think of a time you overlooked your own faults but magnified someone else's?
3. What three things do you condemn yourself for the most?
4. What three things would you like God to help you walk away from?
5. Which one of those things can you start walking away from today?

EIGHT

THE MAN WHO MADE GOD STOP

Now they came to Jericho. As He went out of Jericho with His disciples and a great multitude, blind Bartimaeus, the son of Timaeus, sat by the road begging. And when he heard that it was Jesus of Nazareth, he began to cry out and say, "Jesus, Son of David, have mercy on me!"

Then many warned him to be quiet; but he cried out all the more, "Son of David, have mercy on me!"

So Jesus stood still and commanded him to be called.

Then they called the blind man, saying to him, "Be of good cheer. Rise, He is calling you."

And throwing aside his garment, he rose and came to Jesus.

So Jesus answered and said to him, "What do you want Me to do for you?"

The blind man said to Him, "Rabboni, that I may receive my sight."

Then Jesus said to him, "Go your way; your faith has made you well." And immediately he received his sight and followed Jesus on the road.

(MARK 10:46–52)

In the 1980 comedy *The Gods Must Be Crazy*, a traveling bushman creates a monkey trap. He digs a hole in a termite mound, while a baboon watches from a distance. The hole is large enough for the animal to stick his hand through but too small for him to pull out his clenched fist. The bushman then places melon seeds inside and waits.

After a while the monkey's curiosity gets the best of him. He goes to the mound and reaches in to pull out the seeds. But he cannot get his arm out of the hole, because he will not let go of the seeds. As the baboon struggles to remove his fist from the hole, the bushman puts a rope around its neck. The monkey was only willing to let go of the seeds after it was too late. This comedy illustrates how we can become trapped by things we should let go of much more quickly in life.

The Church of the Nativity in Bethlehem is also revealing. It was built over the traditional birthplace of Jesus. It has a tiny door, called the Door of Humility. To enter, worshippers must stoop down. There is a legend the doorframe was built this way to ensure that everyone who enters will bow before they enter the holy place.

We all have opportunities to encounter God, but the greatest opportunities tend to require us to exhibit high levels of humility before we can fully experience them. The more we refuse to bow from our hearts, the more we bump our heads against the wall until we do.

In the verses that follow, we are going to watch a blind man avoid both the monkey trap and skillfully navigate through the tiny door. He was not a studied theologian, priest, prophet, or even a disciple, yet the Bible says this about Bartimaeus: "So Jesus stood still and commanded him to be called." What is so amazing in this story is not that this man cried out to Jesus for help; that is what we expect beggars to do. What's mind blowing is the fact that Jesus stopped for him.

Now they came to Jericho.

This happened in the vicinity of the famed city whose impregnable walls once stood roughly eighty feet high and six feet wide. More than a thousand years earlier, Joshua—Moses' successor and the commander of God's army—had caused those walls to come tumbling down.

Now, as Jesus again walked through Jericho, walls again would come down, but these walls were not made of stone. These walls were far more stubborn. They were in the hearts and minds of the people following Jesus.

As He went out of Jericho with His disciples and a great multitude

Jesus had served the people of Israel for about three and a half years. The air was thick with the excitement of revolutionary ideas. Words were spoken and miracles were performed, and the multitudes would never be going back to religion as usual. A major paradigm shift was occurring in popular thinking, all due to the controversial carpenter from Galilee.

Jesus departed Jericho with a growing entourage of curiosity seekers and followers. He was preparing for His final entry into Jerusalem. Death loomed less than two weeks away. His disciples opposed and could not fully comprehend His statements predicting the cross He soon would be nailed to (Matthew 16:22; Luke 18:34). Their deep desire to see the full, immediate manifestation of the global kingdom of God almost completely blurred their lenses—until after the resurrection. Jesus felt more and more alone in His understanding of His mission, particularly as it neared its end.

Countless self-consuming thoughts would have filled a lesser mind. Instead, in His characteristic and radical unselfishness, Jesus stopped for a final man before reaching Jerusalem. This would be the last healing He would perform before His final entry into the city to face the cross. The last words and deeds of a person reveal a lot about that person's true priorities.

Blind Bartimaeus, the son of Timaeus

At this point we are introduced to a blind beggar named Bartimaeus. Most people would have ignored this man. He was one of the many thousands of needy, destitute people who constantly roamed the streets. After all, Jesus had already done so much. He had nothing else to prove to the crowd by stopping. Conventional thinking would advise Him to reserve His strength for the confrontation that lay ahead.

To capture the spirit of the encounter, the inspired gospel writer went further. He lets us know this man was not viewed by Jesus as just another statistic. He was someone's child, "the son of Timaeus." Everyone comes from somewhere. We each have a story and are fighting lifelong battles that few others fully understand.

Sat by the road begging.

Bartimaeus had two problems: he was blind and he was poor. The first begat the latter. The ancient Chinese philosopher Confucius observed that in a well-governed country, poverty is something to be ashamed of. In a badly governed country, wealth is something to be ashamed of.[1] In this case, poverty was nothing Bartimaeus should have been ashamed of.

Bartimaeus was not on the sidelines because he was unwilling to work but because of his inability to see. A lack of vision will impact your life more than you can imagine!

And when he heard that it was Jesus of Nazareth, he began to cry out

Living off the charity of strangers was humiliating, an indignity Bartimaeus no longer wanted to bear. Although he was physically blind, his heart (spiritual vision) could see well enough to recognize God when He showed up. Helen Keller famously said, "The only thing worse than being blind is having sight but no vision."[2]

Bartimaeus had heard that Jesus of Nazareth was passing by. The fact this man could not use his eyes did not stop him from using his voice. God always leaves us with something. Your feet may not work, but maybe your hands do. You may not have been born rich, but you were born able to work. You may not have had a lot of people ask you out, but you don't need a lot, only the right one. We don't always have all that we desire, but if we will work with what we have, we will be amazed at what we can do.

And say, "Jesus, Son of David, have mercy on me!"

It is interesting to note that Bartimaeus called Jesus the Son of David. This was a messianic title taken from the Old Testament that foretold the kingdom that Jesus would initiate (2 Samuel 7:12–16). While

Bartimaeus may not have had an extensive knowledge of God's Word due to his blindness, he knew enough Scripture to recognize Jesus as the Son of David and the fulfillment of Old Testament prophecy. We don't have to be scholars to recognize God. If by nature a sheep can distinguish and identify the voice of its shepherd, surely we have adequate innate wiring to recognize the voice of our Shepherd.

Then many warned him to be quiet

Obstacles are put in our paths to determine how much we want what's on the other side of them. Bartimaeus had heard about the many things Jesus did. He was not going to let anything get in the way of his once-in-a-lifetime moment with Jesus. And you shouldn't either!

The crowd did not think this beggar was worthy of Jesus' time and attention. Some people may feel the same way about you and me. Bartimaeus did not fail at his tiny door. He was willing to face whatever ridicule and humiliation were required to walk through his door to Jesus. Sometimes, we must starve and sacrifice our egos so Jesus can feed our souls.

Jesus told a story of two other men at the tiny door:

Two men went up to the temple to pray, one a Pharisee and the other a tax collector. The Pharisee stood and prayed thus with himself, "God, I thank You that I am not like other men—extortioners, unjust, adulterers, or even as this tax collector. I fast twice a week; I give tithes of all that I possess." And the tax collector, standing afar off, would not so much as raise his eyes to heaven, but beat his breast, saying, "God, be merciful to me a sinner!" I tell you, this man went down to his house justified rather than the other; for everyone who exalts himself will be humbled, and he who humbles himself will be exalted. (Luke 18:10–14)

Martial artist and author Bohdi Sanders said, "Most would be horrified if they saw not their faces, but their true character, in the mirror every morning."[3]

But he cried out all the more, "Son of David, have mercy on me!"

Blind Bartimaeus cried out to Jesus based on the Lord's goodness, kindness, and mercy, not his own. He did not compare himself to anyone else to qualify for Jesus' attention. Putting someone else down never makes you any taller. Start crying out to God based on His merits and not your own. Then watch Him do for you what He did for Bartimaeus.

Most people today would have given up and retreated back to the side of the road, saying to themselves, "I give up. Nobody understands me, nobody loves me, and everybody is out to get me." Not Bartimaeus. He only yelled louder. If you fuel your journey with the opinions of others, you are going to run out of gas.[4]

So Jesus stood still and commanded him to be called.

Jesus was on His way to the most important event in human history, His cross, and yet He stopped for this man. A poor, blind man armed with only heartfelt hope and faith made the Creator of the universe stop. The New Testament teaches that Jesus is the same yesterday, today, and forever (Hebrews 13:8). This means if He did it then, He will do it again!

There are at least three major reasons why Jesus stopped for Bartimaeus, and when we apply the same principles to our situations, He will stop for you and me.

1. Bartimaeus approached Jesus in light of what Scripture said about Him. He appealed to Him as Savior and entreated Him based upon the messianic promises.
2. He petitioned Jesus, not based on his own righteousness but because of Jesus' grace and mercy. Bartimaeus deserved nothing but did not let this stop Him from going to Jesus for everything.
3. When he encountered opposition, Bartimaeus did not give up. He dug in and only shouted louder. As Albert Einstein observed, "Great spirits have always encountered violent opposition from mediocre minds."[5]

Then they called the blind man, saying to him, "Be of good cheer. Rise, He is calling you."

The people who just a few minutes earlier had told Bartimaeus to be quiet suddenly began encouraging him. Crowds are so fickle. They can hate you one minute and love you the next. A great man once said, "First, they ignore you, then they laugh at you, then they fight you, then you win."[6] Guard against letting small minds distract you from your larger purpose!

And throwing aside his garment, he rose and came to Jesus.

Bartimaeus immediately threw off his garment and ran to Jesus. By throwing off his cloak, the blind man also threw away his livelihood.

His cloak not only kept him warm at night, but it was what he laid across his lap to collect alms. Bartimaeus refused to get caught in the monkey trap. He realized that to hold on to what's important you must first open your hand and let go.[7]

Biblical Hebrew has no word for a professional beggar. The law of Moses made provisions for the poor but not for a career panhandler. This man's lifestyle was so far below the aspirations God had for His people that Moses never addressed its possibility. Instead of holding on to a handful, he let go and ran toward the pressed-down, shaken-together, and running-over mercy he obviously believed was in Jesus (Luke 6:38).

Running with an outer garment was like a woman trying to run in a dress today. Bartimaeus did not want anything to slow him down or trip him up. He could not allow anything to get in the way of his moment with Jesus.

Think about this. Once Bartimaeus threw his robe aside, there was no guarantee he would ever get it back. After all, he was blind. How could he be sure he would ever find it again? It could have easily been trampled or stolen.

The outer garment was all the poor man had to keep warm on a cold night. But Bartimaeus risked all he had. Sometimes burning a bridge is not a bad thing. It prevents you from going back to the place you should never have been.

So Jesus answered and said to him, "What do you want Me to do for you?"

What you are willing to let go of and leave behind often determines how much God gives back to you. Bartimaeus abandoned himself to

Jesus, and Jesus responded by abandoning Himself for Bartimaeus. Imagine the Creator of the universe stopping for you and asking what you want Him to do for you. If you want to get everything God has for you, you have to be willing to go all out. Don't settle for half measures unless you can be satisfied with half the results.

The blind man said to Him, "Rabboni, that I may receive my sight."

Bartimaeus addressed Jesus differently here than he did in the previous verses. The term "Rabboni" is Aramaic. It means *teacher*, but what is more important, it was used to signify the close relationship between a rabbi and his student.[8]

A rabbinic student's relationship to his master was amazing. Listen to what the Mishna says about a disciple's relationship to his teacher:

> If his lost object and his father's lost object [are to be attended to], his lost object takes precedence; his own lost object and his teacher's lost object, his own takes precedence; his father's lost object and his teacher's lost object, his teacher's takes precedence, because his father brought him into this world, but his teacher, who taught him wisdom, brings him to live [in] the world to come.

Such incredible value was placed on your rabbi that it even exceeded your commitment to your father and family.

> But if his father is no less a scholar than his teacher, then his father's loss takes precedence.

The only way your father could take priority is if he knew the Bible as well as your rabbi or pastor:

> If his father and his teacher are in captivity, he must first ransom his teacher, and only afterwards his father—unless his father is himself a scholar and then he must first ransom his father.[9]

It was a different world. A rabbi was not only loved but feared. Bartimaeus was willing to let go of everything past and present to ensure his relationship with Jesus would grow stronger.

> **Then Jesus said to him, "Go your way; your faith has made you well." And immediately he received his sight and followed Jesus on the road.**

This is important! Bartimaeus's recovery was not only up to Jesus but was also dependent on his faith. Martin Luther aptly described Christianity as simply one beggar telling other beggars where to find bread.[10] And when you truly taste this bread, you will be willing to leave behind everything you previously valued for even the smallest bite.

My Story

My journey has been full of tiny doors and monkey traps. Would I humble myself and persevere through opposition and my own doubts? Could I find the courage to let go of what was in my hand for what God had in His hand for me farther down the road? The greatest enemy of your next success is always your last success.

Some people are born with spectacular gifts and can perform exceptionally with little effort. But there are many, like me, who are given only a modest amount of natural talent for their life's assignment. It is only through prayer, hard work, and grueling perseverance that we can make a positive impact on our communities and on those we love.

Think about this question: If God offered to give you a penny and doubled it every day for a month or a single check for $1 million and gave you only a few seconds to answer, which would you take? If you are like me, you would jump at the million dollars. But watch what happens to the insignificant penny over thirty days:

Day 1	$0.01	Day 16	$327.68
Day 2	$0.02	Day 17	$655.36
Day 3	$0.04	Day 18	$1,310.72
Day 4	$0.08	Day 19	$2,621.44
Day 5	$0.16	Day 20	$5,242.88
Day 6	$0.32	Day 21	$10,485.76
Day 7	$0.64	Day 22	$20,971.52
Day 8	$1.28	Day 23	$41,943.04
Day 9	$2.56	Day 24	$83,886.08
Day 10	$5.12	Day 25	$167,772.16
Day 11	$10.24	Day 26	$335,544.32
Day 12	$20.48	Day 27	$671,088.64
Day 13	$40.96	Day 28	$1,342,177.28
Day 14	$81.92	Day 29	$2,684,354.56
Day 15	$163.84	Day 30	$5,368,709.12

God may have given others million-dollar gifts from the beginning, but the Lord in His wisdom only offered this young introvert a penny's worth. At first, I felt frustrated and disappointed. At times I was intimidated by the more spectacular gifts God gave others. But with time I understood and appreciated the value and wisdom of my penny.

My penny did not double every day as in the illustration above. My days were more like years. I was nineteen when the Lord showed up in my dormitory room, twenty when I gave my life to the carpenter from Galilee, and it would be twenty-five to thirty years before I could begin to see the fruit of God's process.

In 2014, after years of developing an incredibly deep root system, it finally paid off. To our total shock Grace Church became one of the fastest-growing churches in the United States, but our story has been a lot like the Chinese bamboo tree. The Chinese bamboo tree begins as a small, hard nut that must be planted in soil, watered, and fertilized daily for five years. If at any time the watering and fertilizing process is stopped, the Chinese bamboo tree will die in the ground. But, if you continue to water and fertilize the seed every day, sometime in that fifth year, the Chinese bamboo tree finally sprouts and, in a six-week period, grows nearly ninety feet. Now the question is, did it grow ninety feet in six weeks or in five years?

The answer is five years. Over time, the tree developed a strong enough root system to sustain its life as it grew during those years. Sometimes a delay is simply time for preparation.

In 2015 we began to outgrow our current facility, so we purchased 11.5 acres of undeveloped land about five minutes from our current property. After we purchased the property, I received a call from my project manager that helped my journey come full circle. He discovered the land we bought and on which we would build our church was once used to house slaves for those who worked the charcoal furnaces of Virginia.

Making this charcoal was tedious and hard work. They cut down trees and slowly burned them in airless pits until all the moisture was removed and all that was left was a pure form of carbon. It was a dirty and dangerous job. Fumes, smoke, and dust covered the workers.

If even a slight spark remained while the slaves peeled away the coal, it would ignite and ruin the whole coal stack and the workers were often burned. Yet the burns were not as painful as the punishment that would come from the slave owners for ruining the precious potential inventory.[11]

On land where these slaves slept, bled, and died, 150 years later God raised up a congregation that would be privileged to share a message of emancipation with the world. I can only imagine the prayers my forebearers prayed as they lay on their hard floors at night, beseeching God for their freedom and the freedom of their children. The young man who once angrily characterized Christianity as a white man's religion can only look to Jesus humbled by God's poetic justice. As the abolitionist Theodore Parker once said, "The arc of the moral universe is long but it bends toward justice."[12]

God never promised our road will be easy. He just promised it will be worth it. In my mind, I was one of the least likely people to be placed in God's service—an introvert, womanizer, and black nationalist; headstrong, proud, and stubborn; selfish and with many life options that never included carrying a cross (Matthew 16:24–26). Yet God's mercy went to work in my life as He stopped by daily, through His Word, to help me heal and grow.

Throughout my life and the lives of the Bible characters we studied together, we discovered that we cannot always calm the storm, but if we calm ourselves, the storm eventually will have to pass!

Your particular sin, objections, and weaknesses may come in a slightly different flavor than mine, but no matter your race, personality type, or particular bent, underneath it all, we are all the same. We are imperfect people in need of our perfect Savior to stop by our situation.

The psalmist said, "He lifted me out of the pit of despair, out of the mud and the mire. He set my feet on solid ground and steadied me as I walked along" (Psalm 40:2 NLT). This certainly captures my journey, and I hope it will soon describe yours.

Martin Luther King Jr. said, "We must accept finite disappointment but never lose infinite hope."[13] If life has taught me anything it is: never waste a good failure! My failures have cost me too much to squander them by not learning from them or sharing them with others. If I could put everything I have written in a nutshell, it would be this: If Jesus so generously stopped for such an unlikely nobody as me, why wouldn't He also stop for you? Right now, call on Him like the characters of this book did, call on Him.

Summary

- A lack of vision will impact you more than you can imagine.
- "Jesus Christ is the same yesterday, today, and forever."
- If you are going to receive anything from Jesus, you will have to be willing to deal with criticism.
- True healing begins within.

- God always has the power; the problem is we often don't have the faith to press through the insults, opposition, and fears to take hold of what the Bible says is ours.

Self-Analysis

1. In what ways have you refused to let your challenges or disabilities dictate what you can have or what you can do?
2. Do you believe God is good all the time or just sometimes? When you are going through hard times, do you see this as God's love and goodness or punishment toward you?
3. When have you allowed what the crowd says to hold you back?
4. Can you make some time today to talk to God with empty hands and see Him asking you, "What do you want Me to do for you?"
5. Have you ever truly run after God with all your might?

ACKNOWLEDGMENTS

Special thanks to Chaplain Barry Black for your advice and challenging me to put this manuscript together. You are a living legend. Damon Davis, you are a true friend, and your input and the support of Legacy Worldwide has been invaluable. Charlie Campbell, you are the *get it done guy* everyone wishes they had on their team. Dr. Cindy Trimm and Bishop Walter Thomas, our conversations have been more impactful than you probably imagined. Dr. Sam Chand, you are the coolest leader's leader on the planet. Thanks for more than a decade of coaching.

Lastly, thank you to the Grace Church staff for holding up my arms as we endeavor to impact as many lives as possible, in this very short season called life.

APPENDIX

The New Testament and Slavery

Slavery existed in the ancient world thousands of years before the first century. The Mesopotamians, Chinese, Egyptians, Greeks, and eventually the Romans all participated in this institution. Unlike the slavery that would develop in the Americas, however, Roman slavery was not based on race.

Slavery in any form is often abusive and degrading. But the slavery in the Roman world was in many ways different from the slavery established in North America. Manumission, the ability of a slave to go free, was common. Roman slaves were generally allowed to work for pay. They could save, and they often bought back their freedom.

Once a slave was manumitted, the person received the full rights of Roman citizenship. They were not allowed to hold office and among the cultural elite there was a stigma associated with once being a slave. But a slave's freeborn child could hold office.[1]

More than a thousand years after the New Testament writing, in the sixteenth through the nineteenth centuries, Europeans began their slave trade long after the start of the Arab African slave trade. The New Testament writers never endorsed or promoted slavery.

Because slavery was so pervasive, the early apostles instructed followers of Jesus how to manage and survive this once universally entrenched institution.

1. Paul advocated for slaves to gain their freedom when possible.

> Were you called while a slave? Do not be concerned about it; but if you can be made free, rather use it. (1 Corinthians 7:21)

> Stay where you were when God called your name. Were you a slave? Slavery is no roadblock to obeying and believing. I don't mean you're stuck and can't leave. If you have a chance at freedom, go ahead and take it. (1 Corinthians 7:21 THE MESSAGE)

2. Kidnapping played such a vital role in the American slave trade that it could not have existed without it. Paul listed the kidnapping of other humans among the most egregious of sins. He called such behavior contrary to sound doctrine and placed those who practiced it in the same category as perjurers and liars.

> Knowing this: that the law is not made for a righteous person, but for the lawless and insubordinate, for the ungodly and for sinners, for the unholy and profane, for murderers of fathers and murderers of mothers, for manslayers, for fornicators, for sodomites, for kidnappers, for liars, for perjurers, and if there is any other thing that is contrary to sound doctrine. (1 Timothy 1:9–10)

3. An entire epistle written by the apostle Paul was dedicated to securing the freedom of a slave named Onesimus. Paul saw the slave as a spiritual equal and even offered to use his own money to pay for this slave's freedom.

If then you count me as a partner, receive him as you would me. But if he has wronged you or owes anything, put that on my account. I, Paul, am writing with my own hand. I will repay—not to mention to you that you owe me even your own self besides. (Philemon v. 17–19)

4. The New Testament strategy was not an armed revolt to liberate slaves but to foster such a high reputation of genuine Christians that the Roman world would soon be won to the faith. Slavery would then become obsolete.

Let as many bondservants as are under the yoke count their own masters worthy of all honor, so that the name of God and His doctrine may not be blasphemed. (1 Timothy 6:1)

5. Until the gospel could transform the Roman world, Scripture gave followers of Jesus very clear instructions about how to represent God's kingdom in the present social order. Many suffered joyfully only because of their confidence that God would one day balance the ledger for every infraction and abuse.

Bondservants, be obedient to those who are your masters according to the flesh, with fear and trembling, in sincerity of heart, as to Christ; not with eyeservice, as men-pleasers, but as bondservants of Christ, doing the will of God from the heart, with goodwill doing service, as to the Lord, and not to men, knowing that whatever good anyone does, he will receive the same from the Lord, whether he is a slave or free. (Ephesians 6:5–8)

6. Paul severely cautioned believing slave owners. He understood that slavery often did as much to degrade the soul of the slave owner, as the slave.

And you, masters, do the same things to them, giving up threaten-ing, knowing that your own Master also is in heaven, and there is no partiality with Him. (Ephesians 6:9)

7. James, in his epistle, noticed social distinctions being made between the slave-owning class ("the rich man") and slaves and peas-ants ("the poor man") and sharply rebuked it.

My brethren, do not hold the faith of our Lord Jesus Christ, the Lord of glory, with partiality. For if there should come into your assembly a man with gold rings, in fine apparel, and there should also come in a poor man in filthy clothes, and you pay attention to the one wearing the fine clothes and say to him, "You sit here in a good place," and say to the poor man, "You stand there," or, "Sit here at my footstool," have you not shown partiality among yourselves, and become judges with evil thoughts?

Listen, my beloved brethren: Has God not chosen the poor of this world to be rich in faith and heirs of the kingdom which He promised to those who love Him? But you have dishonored the poor man. Do not the rich oppress you and drag you into the courts? Do they not blaspheme that noble name by which you are called? (James 2:1–7)

8. Slavery that existed at the time of the writing of the New Testament was not established under the guise of Christianizing or civilizing the enslaved. It was the reverse. The slave population of the first century was predominately Christian, and it was often the slaveholders who were not. It was the slaves who won their masters to Christianity and not vice versa.

Servants, be submissive to your masters with all fear, not only to the good and gentle, but also to the harsh. For this is commendable, if because of conscience toward God one endures grief, suffering wrongfully. For what credit is it if, when you are beaten for your faults, you take it patiently? But when you do good and suffer, if you take it patiently, this is commendable before God. For to this you were called, because Christ also suffered for us, leaving us an example, that you should follow His steps:

> "Who committed no sin,
> Nor was deceit found in His mouth";

> who, when He was reviled, did not revile in return; when He suffered, He did not threaten, but committed Himself to Him who judges righteously. (1 Peter 2:18–23)

9. The New Testament church totally transcended the social order of the day. The gospel offered a totally new relationship with God and one another that totally transcended gender, race, education, and social status. Everyone became equal sisters and brothers in the family of God.

> There is neither Jew nor Greek, there is neither slave nor free, there is neither male nor female; for you are all one in Christ Jesus. (Galatians 3:28)

NOTES

Chapter 1: The Woman Who Made God Stop

1. C. S. Lewis, *Mere Christianity: A Revised and Enlarged Edition, with a New Introduction, of the Three Books, The Case for Christianity, Christian Behavior, and Beyond Personality* (New York: Macmillan), 195.

2. Edward W. Desmond, "Interview with Mother Teresa: A Pencil in the Hand of God," *Time*, December 4, 1989; see Luke 6:25.

3. C. J. Ellicott, *A Bible Commentary for English Readers* (Charleston, SC: Nabu Press, 2011).

4. If the Shroud of Turin is what some claim it to be, the shroud suggests Jesus may have been around five feet nine inches, which would make Jesus very tall for this time.

5. Cunningham Geikie, *The Life and Words of Christ*, 2 vols. (New York: D. Appleton and Company, 1877).

6. Fannie Lou Haman, August 22, 1964, at the Democratic National Convention in Atlantic City.

7. Henry Kaiser, *Congressional Record: Proceedings and Debates of the Congress*, vol. 113, part 18, p. 1969.

8. See Mark Twain, Letter to an unnamed recipient in Buffalo, NY, August 28, 1908, in *Mark Twain's Letters, 1907–1910*, vol. 6, comp. Albert Bigelow Paine (New York: Harper, 1917).

9. Penny Marshall, Tom Hanks, Geena Davis, Madonna, Lori Petty, Rosie O'Donnell, Jon Lovitz, et al., *A League of Their Own* (Culver City, CA: Columbia Tristar Home Video, 2004).

Chapter 2: The Man Who Made God Look Up

1. James Edward Stroud, *The Knights Templar and the Protestant Reformation* (Maitland, FL: Xulon Press, 2011), 162. Some argue, however, that Gandhi (1869–1948) never said this.

2. Craig Groeschel, *Liking Jesus: Intimacy and Contentment in a Selfie-Centered World* (Grand Rapids, MI: Zondervan, 2018), section 1.3, https://www.google.com/books/edition/Liking_Jesus/s4EoDwAA QBAJ?hl=en&gbpv=1&dq=chuck+swindoll+life+is+10+percent+what +happens+to+you+and+90+percent+how+you+respond&pg=PT19 &printsec=frontcover.

3. Dr. Purushothaman, *Words of Wisdom* (vol. 42): *1001 Quotes & Quotations*, p. 42.

4. Generally attributed to Seneca, but no original source located.

5. Harper Lee, *To Kill a Mockingbird*, 40th Anniversary Edition (NY: HarperCollins, 1999), 257.

6. Dr. Warren R. Weissman, *The Power of Infinite Love* (Hay House, Inc., 2007), 30.

7. Frederick Buechner, *The Final Beast* (New York: Seabury Press, 1967).

Chapter 3: The Man God Looked For

1. Cal Fussman, "What I've Learned: Christopher Reeve," *Esquire*, January 29, 2007, http://www.esquire.com/entertainment/interviews /a1992/esq0104-jan-superheroes-1/.

2. Oswald Chambers, *The Oswald Chambers Devotional Reader: 52 Weekly Themes*, ed. Harry Verploegh (Nashville: Oliver Nelson, 1990), 79.

3. Jonathan Lipnick, "The Gates of the Sheep and Lion," Israel Institute of Biblical Studies, May 21, 2016, https://blog.israelbiblicalstudies.com /holy-land-studies/where-is-the-gate-of-the-sheep/.

4. David Maraniss, *When Pride Still Mattered: A Life of Vince Lombardi* (New York: Simon & Schuster, 2000), 365.

5. Frederick Douglass, "Self-Made Men" speech, 1859, Monadnock Valley Press, http://monadnock.net/douglass/self-made-men.html.

6. Aeschylus, *Seven Against Thebes*, lines 224–225.

7. Charles H. Spurgeon, *The Sword and the Trowel*, November 1, 1876.

8. Richard Cecil and John Newton, *The Works of the Rev. John Newton* (R. Carter, 1844), 355.

9. Francis Bacon, *Bacon's Essays: With Annotations by Richard Whately*, 3rd Ed. (London: J. W. Parker, 1857), 380.

10. John R. W. Stott, *The Cross of Christ* (Downers Grove, IL: InterVarsity, 1986), 159.

11. Arnold A. Dallimore, *Spurgeon: A New Biography* (Edinburgh: Banner of Truth, 1987).

Chapter 4: When God Stopped By

1. Quoted in Correlli Barnett, *The Swordbearers: Studies in Supreme Command in the First World War* (London: Eyre and Spottiswoode, 1963), 35.

2. Bernard Zlotowitz and David Kasakove, "Jewish Wedding Practices: Surprising Origins and Reform Innovations," Reform Judaism, https://reformjudaism.org/jewish-wedding-practices-surprising-origins -and-reform-innovations.

3. Abraham P. Bloch, *The Biblical and Historical Background of Jewish Customs and Ceremonies* (New York: Ktav Publishing House, 1980), 32.

4. "Ancient Marriage: Ancient Manners and Customs, Daily Life, Cultures, Bible Lands," Bible History Online, http://www.bible-history .com/biblestudy/marriage.html.

5. Maurice Lamm, "Wine at the Jewish Wedding," http://www.chabad.org /library/article_cdo/aid/481775/jewish/Wine.htm.

6. R. A. Baker, "Wine in the Ancient World," Early Church History— CH101, 2007, http://churchhistory101.com/wine-alcohol-bible.php.

7. Charles W. Draper, Chad Brand, and Archie England, eds., *Holman Illustrated Bible Dictionary* (Nashville: B&H, 2003), 1664.

8. C. S. Lewis, *Mere Christianity* (San Francisco: HarperSanFrancisco, 2001), 51–52.

9. *Debates and Proceedings of the Constitutional Convention of the State of Illinois: Convened at the City of Springfield, Tuesday, December 13, 1869*, (Springfield, IL: E. L. Merritt & Brother, Printers to the Convention, 1870), 234.

10. Quoted in George Washington Burnap, *The Sphere and Duties of Woman*, 3rd ed. (Baltimore: J. Murphy; Philadelphia: J. Fullerton, 1848), Lecture 4.

11. *Music: The Definitive Visual History* (United Kingdom: DK, 2013), 232.

12. Abraham Joshua Heschel, National Conference of Religion and Race, January 14, 1963.

13. Research Release in Faith and Christianity, "The State of the Church 2016," September 15, 2016, https://www.barna.com/research/state -church-2016/.

14. Martin Luther King Jr., "Drum Major Instinct," February 4, 1968, Ebenezer Baptist Church, Atlanta, GA, https://kinginstitute.stanford .edu/king-papers/documents/drum-major-instinct-sermon-delivered -ebenezer-baptist-church.

15. Charles H. Spurgeon, *Lectures to My Students* (Peabody, MA: Hendrickson, 2010), 59–60, 64.

Chapter 5: God Stopped to Get In

1. *Catfish*, dir. Henry Joost and Ariel Schulman (Beverly Hills and University City, CA: Relativity Media and Rogue Pictures, 2010), https://www.imdb.com/title/tt1584016/quotes?ref_=tt_ql_trv_4.

2. I cannot claim this insight as my own, but I do not know from whom I heard it or where I might have read it.

3. Credited to John A. Shedd, *Salt from My Attic* (Portland, ME: Mosher Press, 1928); see also Fred R. Shapiro, ed., *The Yale Book of Quotations* (New Haven: Yale University Press, 2006), 705.

4. Chuck Konselman and Cary Solomon, *God's Not Dead 2*, dir. Harold Cronk (Scottsdale, AZ: Pure Flix, 2016).

5. Credited to author and motivational speaker Jack Canfield.

6. Credited to Rick Warren, pastor of Saddleback Church, Lake Forest, California.

7. Dr. Leigh-Davis, *Quote Book: Quotes from Powerful Women about Power* (CreateSpace Independent Publishing Platform, 2012), 11. Ruth Gordon, credited with this quote, is an award-winning actress and writer.

8. This insight is often attributed to Franklin D. Roosevelt.

9. Bob Loyce Moore is an American session musician, orchestra leader, and bassist who was a member of the Nashville A-Team during the 1950s and 1960s. Read more at https://www.quotetab.com/quotes /by-bob-moore#lm44v5RqQh0QqtKe.99.

10. James Harold Doyle, *The Call of Education. United States of America* (Doyle, 1921), 217.

11. Michael Edmondson, PhD, *Navigate the Chaos: 365 Strategies for Personal Growth and Professional Development* (Lulu Press, 2017), 168.

12. Although often attributed to Abraham Lincoln, this sentiment likely comes from Frank Crane, "New Year's Resolutions," *Syracuse Herald*, January 1, 1914, https://quoteinvestigator.com/2012/10/20/happy-minds/.

13. Carter G. Woodson, *The Mis-Education of the Negro* (Washington, DC: Associated Publishers, 1933), 71.

14. Edward Mote, "The Solid Rock," 1834.

15. Jane E. Harber, *Have a Miracle: Experiencing Rest and Refreshing in This Harried, Hurried World* (Oklahoma: Tate Publishing, 2010), 150.

16. Watchman Nee, *The Finest of the Wheat: Selected Excerpts from the Published Works of Watchman Nee* (Christian Fellowship Publishers, 1993), 395.

Chapter 6: Lepers Who Did Not Stop

1. Beth Moore, *Jesus, the One and Only* (Nashville: Broadman & Holman, 2002), 203–4.

2. *Strong's Concordance*, no. 2962, *kurios*, http://biblehub.com/greek/2962.htm.

3. William George Jordan, *The Power of Truth; Individual Problems and Possibilities* (Brentano's, 1916), 25.

4. Some attribute the quote to Steven Furtick, but it is not definitive; the author is unknown.

5. John B. Gilmour, *Strategic Disagreement: Stalemate in American Politics* (University of Pittsburgh Press, 1995), 132.

6. Robert Andrews, *Famous Lines* (New York City: Columbia University Press, 1993), 245.

7. *Words of Wisdom (vol. 14): 1001 Quotes & Quotations* (Centre For Human Perfection, 2014), 141.

Chapter 7: The People God Had to Stop

1. All quotations in this section are from Frederick Douglass, *Narrative of the Life of Frederick Douglass, an American Slave* (Boston: Anti-Slavery Office, 1845), http://www.gutenberg.org/files/23/23-h/23-h.htm.

2. Charles W. Draper, Chad Brand, and Archie England, eds., *Holman Illustrated Bible Dictionary* (Nashville: B&H, 2003), 1219.

3. Martin Luther, Helmut Lehman, *Luther's Works: Sermons on St. John: Volume 24 of Luther's Works* (Concordia Publishing House, 1986), 89.

4. Quoted in Joseph P. Lash, *Helen and Teacher: The Story of Helen Keller and Anne Sullivan Macy* (New York: Delacorte Press, 1980), 489.

5. T. F. Hodge, *From Within I Rise: Spiritual Triumph over Death and Conscious Encounters with "The Divine Presence"* (Frederick, MD: PublishAmerica, 2009).

6. This quotation is often attributed to John Wesley, but there is no evidence to support this.

7. Draper, Brand, and England, *Holman Illustrated Bible Dictionary*, 1287 and 1452; 2 Corinthians 3:6.

8. Benjamin Franklin, *Poor Richard's Almanack* (Waterloo, IA: U. S. C. Publishing Co., 1914), no. 179, https://archive.org/stream/poor richardsalma00franrich/poorrichardsalma00franrich_djvu.txt.

9. Draper, Brand, and England, *Holman Illustrated Bible Dictionary*, 1445.

10. Attributed to John Bradford in Bradford, *The Writings of John Bradford*, ed. Aubrey Townsend, 2 vols. (Cambridge: Cambridge University Press, 1848–53), 1:xliii.

11. I cannot claim this insight as my own, but I do not know from whom I heard it or where I might have read it.

12. *Fresh Illustrations for Preaching and Teaching: From Leadership Journal* (Baker Books, 2000), 82.

13. James P. Long, "The 2013 Outreach 100," *Outreach Magazine*, September 11, 2013; James P. Long, "The 2014 Outreach 100," *Outreach Magazine*, September 2014.

Chapter 8: The Man Who Made God Stop

1. *The Analects of Confucius*, 8.13.3.

2. Tim McConnell, *Small Steps on a Long Journey: A Collection of Thoughtful Devotions* (Xlibris, 2010), 232.

3. Bohdi Sanders.

4. Steve Maraboli, *Unapologetically You: Reflections on Life and the Human Experience* (Port Washington, NY: A Better Today Publishing, 2013).

5. In Albert Einstein to Morris Raphael Cohen, March 11, 1940, Albert Einstein Collection, 1921–1954, University of Chicago Library.

6. This quotation is often attributed to Mahatma Gandhi (beginning with the proceedings of a 1982 Workshop in Nonviolence Institute gathering), but there is no evidence to confirm this. The earliest claim goes to Nicholas Klein, who is credited with a variant of the quotation in a May 1918 speech at a meeting of the Amalgamated Clothing Workers of America, https://www.apnews.com/afs:Content:2315880316.

7. Sridhar Vasudevan, *Multidisciplinary Management of Chronic Pain: A Practical Guide for Clinicians* (Germany: Springer International Publishing, 2015), 8.

8. Charles W. Draper, Chad Brand, and Archie England, eds., *Holman Illustrated Bible Dictionary* (Nashville: B&H, 2003), 1360.

9. Mishnah Bava Metsi'a 2:11, https://www.sefaria.org/Mishnah_Bava_Metzia.2.11?lang=bi.

10. Paul Copan, *That's Just Your Interpretation: Responding to Skeptics Who Challenge Your Faith* (Baker, 2001), 28.

11. Victor R. Rolando, "Making Charcoal," *Historic Roots* 4, no. 1 (April 1999): 15–21, https://vermonthistory.org/images/stories/articles/historic roots/makingcharcoal.pdf.

12. Theodore Parker, *Ten Sermons of Religion* (Little, Brown and Company, 1855), 84–85, https://quoteinvestigator.com/2012/11/15/arc-of-universe/.

13. Martin Luther King, "Proper Sense of Priorities," Feb. 6. 1968, Washington, DC, http://www.aavw.org/special_features/speeches _speech_king04.html.

Appendix

1. "Slaves and Freedom," *The Roman Empire: In the First Century*, PBS. org, http://www.pbs.org/empires/romans/empire/slaves_freemen.html.

ABOUT THE AUTHOR

D r. Derek Grier is the founding pastor of Grace Church in Dumfries, Virginia, which began with twelve people and currently has more than five thousand members. His radio and television ministry reach millions around the globe. He is also the founder of several educational training and outreach programs, including Virginia Bible College, Renaissance Leadership Network, DGM Growth Lab, and Project Promise.

BECOME PART OF A COMMUNITY OF LIKE-MINDED LEADERS WHO DESIRE TO SEE GOD'S KINGDOM ADVANCE!

Thank you for taking the opportunity to read my book "When God Stops." It is my sincere hope that this book served as tool to help energize your relationship with God and see Him move in your situation!

I would also like to personally help you develop your leadership and organizational skills through the Renaissance Leadership Network (RLN).

Please go to **RLNleadership.com/special** to learn more about how RLN is coaching world-class servant-leaders in every arena, as well as a **special offer** on how you can become a member.

You can also **GET A FREE COPY** of my *RLN Manifesto* featuring coaching sessions from today's top leadership experts and consultants.

CLAIM YOUR FREE COPY AT
RLNLEADERSHIP.COM/SPECIAL